BASEBALL CARDS

LOS ANGELES

Text by
Red Foley

PRICE STERN SLOAN
Los Angeles

Published by Price Stern Sloan, Inc.
360 North La Cienega Boulevard, Los Angeles, California 90048

ISBN 0-8431-2473-3

Officially licensed by Major League Baseball

Official Licensee

© 1988 MLBPA
© MSA

An MBKA Production

Printed and bound in Hong Kong.

TEAM LEADERS

Home Runs
1958 - Gil Hodges, Charlie Neal (22)
1959 - Gil Hodges (25)
1960 - Frank Howard (23)
1961 - John Roseboro (18)
1962 - Frank Howard (31)
1963 - Frank Howard (28)
1964 - Frank Howard (24)
1965 - Lou Johnson, Jim Lefebvre (12)
1966 - Jim Lefebvre (24)
1967 - Al Ferrara (16)
1968 - Len Gabrielson (10)
1969 - Andy Kosco (19)
1970 - Billy Grabarkewitz (17)
1971 - Dick Allen (23)
1972 - Willie Davis, Frank Robinson (19)
1973 - Joe Ferguson (25)
1974 - Jim Wynn (32)
1975 - Ron Cey (25)
1976 - Ron Cey (23)
1977 - Steve Garvey (33)
1978 - Reggie Smith (29)
1979 - Ron Cey, Steve Garvey,
       Davey Lopes (28)
1980 - Dusty Baker (29)
1981 - Ron Cey (13)
1982 - Pedro Guerrero (32)
1983 - Pedro Guerrero (32)
1984 - Mike Marshall (21)
1985 - Pedro Guerrero (33)
1986 - Franklin Stubbs (23)
1987 - Pedro Guerrero (27)
1988 - Kirk Gibson (25)

Runs Batted In
Carl Furillo (83)
Duke Snider (88)
Norm Larker (78)
Wally Moon (88)
Tommy Davis (153)
Tommy Davis (88)
Tommy Davis (86)
Ron Fairly (70)
Jim Lefebvre (74)
Ron Fairly (55)
Tom Haller (53)
Andy Kosco (74)
Wes Parker (111)
Dick Allen (90)
Willie Davis (79)
Joe Ferguson (88)
Steve Garvey (111)
Ron Cey (101)
Ron Cey, Steve Garvey (80)
Steve Garvey (115)
Steve Garvey (113)
Steve Garvey (110)

Steve Garvey (106)
Steve Garvey (64)
Pedro Guerrero (100)
Pedro Guerrero (103)
Pedro Guerrero (72)
Mike Marshall (95)
Bill Madlock (60)
Pedro Guerrero (89)
Mike Marshall (82)

Batting Average
Duke Snider (.312)
Duke Snider (.308)
Norm Larker (.323)
Wally Moon (.328)
Tommy Davis (.346)
Tommy Davis (.326)
Willie Davis (.294)
Maury Wills (.286)
Willie Davis (.284)
Al Ferrara (.277)
Tom Haller (.285)
Willie Davis (.311)
Wes Parker (.319)
Willie Davis (.309)
Manny Mota (.323)
Manny Mota (.314)
Bill Buckner (.314)
Steve Garvey (.319)
Steve Garvey (.317)
Reggie Smith (.307)
Steve Garvey (.316)
Steve Garvey (.315)

Steve Garvey (.304)
Dusty Baker (.320)
Pedro Guerrero (.304)
Pedro Guerrero (.298)
Pedro Guerrero (.303)
Pedro Guerrero (.320)
Steve Sax (.332)
Pedro Guerrero (.338)
Kirk Gibson (.290)

Wins	Strikeouts	Earned Run Average
1958 - Johnny Podres (13)	Johnny Podres (143)	Johnny Podres (3.73)
1959 - Don Drysdale (17)	Don Drysdale (242)	Don Drysdale (3.45)
1960 - Don Drysdale (15)	Don Drysdale (246)	Don Drysdale (2.84)
1961 - Sandy Koufax, Johnny Podres (18)	Sandy Koufax (269)	Sandy Koufax (3.52)
1962 - Don Drysdale (25)	Don Drysdale (232)	Sandy Koufax (2.54)
1963 - Sandy Koufax (25)	Sandy Koufax (306)	Sandy Koufax (1.88)
1964 - Sandy Koufax (19)	Don Drysdale (237)	Sandy Koufax (1.74)
1965 - Sandy Koufax (26)	Sandy Koufax (382)	Sandy Koufax (2.04)
1966 - Sandy Koufax (27)	Sandy Koufax (317)	Sandy Koufax (1.73)
1967 - Claude Osteen (17)	Don Drysdale (196)	Ron Perranoski (2.45)
1968 - Don Drysdale (14)	Bill Singer (227)	Don Drysdale (2.15)
1969 - Claude Osteen, Bill Singer (20)	Bill Singer (246)	Bill Singer (2.34)
1970 - Claude Osteen (16)	Don Sutton (201)	Sandy Vance (3.13)
1971 - Al Downing (20)	Don Sutton (194)	Jim Brewer (1.89)
1972 - Claude Osteen (20)	Don Sutton (207)	Don Sutton (2.08)
1973 - Don Sutton (18)	Don Sutton (200)	Don Sutton (2.42)
1974 - Andy Messersmith (20)	Andy Messersmith (221)	Mike Marshall (2.42)
1975 - Andy Messersmith (19)	Andy Messersmith (213)	Andy Messersmith (2.29)
1976 - Don Sutton (21)	Don Sutton (161)	Charlie Hough (2.20)
1977 - Tommy John (20)	Burt Hooton (153)	Burt Hooton (2.62)
1978 - Burt Hooton (19)	Don Sutton (154)	Bob Welch (2.03)
1979 - Rick Sutcliffe (17)	Don Sutton (146)	Burt Hooton (2.97)
1980 - Jerry Reuss (18)	Bob Welch (141)	Don Sutton (2.21)
1981 - Fernando Valenzuela (13)	Fernando Valenzuela (180)	Burt Hooton (2.28)
1982 - Fernando Valenzuela (19)	Fernando Valenzuela (199)	Steve Howe (2.08)
1983 - Fernando Valenzuela Bob Welch (15)	Fernando Valenzuela (189)	Bob Welch (2.65)
1984 - Bob Welch (13)	Fernando Valenzuela (240)	Alejandro Pena (2.48)
1985 - Orel Hershiser (19)	Fernando Valenzuela (208)	Orel Hershiser (2.03)
1986 - Fernando Valenzuela (21)	Fernando Valenzuela (242)	Fernando Valenzuela (3.14)
1987 - Orel Hershiser (16)	Bob Welch (196)	Orel Hershiser (3.06)
1988 - Orel Hershiser (23)	Tim Leary (180)	Orel Hershiser (2.26)

1952

The National League pennant that had eluded them the previous two years became a reality for the Dodgers in 1952. Manager Chuck Dressen's club, leading the league since June 1, finished four and a half lengths in front of the pursuing Giants.

Jackie Robinson (.308), George Shuba (.305) and Duke Snider (.303) comprised a trio of .300-hitters while Roy Campanella had 22 homers and 97 runs batted in. Gil Hodges hit 32 homers and drove home 102. Pee Wee Reese led the league in stolen bases, swiping 30 in 35 attempts.

The pitching staff, though lacking a 20-game winner, was headed by Rookie of the Year Joe Black. The righthander was 15-4 with a 2.15 earned run average. Veteran lefty Preacher Roe wound up 11-2, while Carl Erskine, who no-hit Chicago in June, was hampered by elbow problems. He finished 14-6 with a 2.70 ERA. In the World Series, in which they faced the Yankees, the Dodgers bowed in seven games.

JOE BLACK

ROCKY BRIDGES

ROY CAMPANELLA

BILLY COX

CHUCK DRESSEN

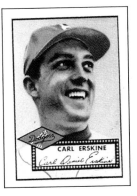
CARL ERSKINE

PHIL HAUGSTAD

BILLY HERMAN

GIL HODGES

CLYDE KING

CLEM LABINE

"COOKIE" LAVAGETTO

BILLY LOES

BOBBY MORGAN

GLENN NELSON

ANDY PAFKO

JAKE PITLER

ERV PALICA

CLARENCE PODBIELAN

PEE WEE REESE

JACKIE ROBINSON

"PREACHER" ROE

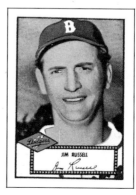

JIM RUSSELL

JOHN RUTHERFORD

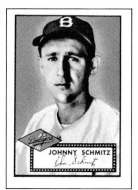
JOHNNY SCHMITZ

GEORGE SHUBA

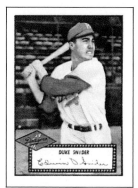
DUKE SNIDER

WAYNE TERWILLIGER

CHRIS VAN CUYK

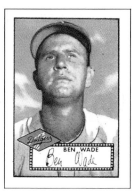
BEN WADE

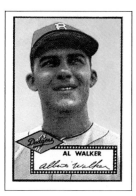
AL WALKER

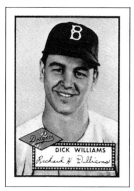
DICK WILLIAMS

1953

A heavy-hitting lineup that featured five .300-hitters enabled the Dodgers to win their second straight pennant in 1953, this one by 13½ games. Roy Campanella, batting .312, banged 41 homers and had 142 RBIs and captured his second MVP award. Duke Snider batted .336 with 42 homers and 126 RBIs.

Carl Furillo, suffering a bone fracture in his left hand in September, was the league's leading hitter at .344, while Gil Hodges hit 31 homers and had 122 RBIs. Jackie Robinson batted .329 and second baseman Jim Gilliam was Rookie of the Year.

Carl Erskine was the pitching leader with a 20-6 mark. Russ Meyer went 15-5. Billy Loes, following a fast start, ended 14-8. Preacher Roe was 11-3, but Joe Black, the 1952 sensation, was restricted by arm ailments to a 6-3 record. For the second straight year the Dodgers challenged the Yankees in the World Series, and were defeated in six games.

Shortly after the Series, the Dodgers announced that Charlie Dressen, because of his insistence on more than a one-year managerial contract, would not return as pilot in 1954.

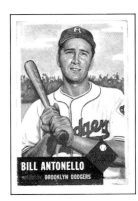

BILL ANTONELLO outfielder BROOKLYN DODGERS

JOE BLACK pitcher Brooklyn Dodgers

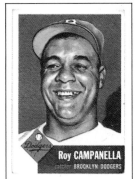

Roy **CAMPANELLA** catcher BROOKLYN DODGERS

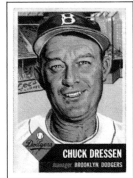

CHUCK DRESSEN manager BROOKLYN DODGERS

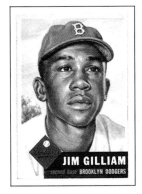

JIM GILLIAM second base BROOKLYN DODGERS

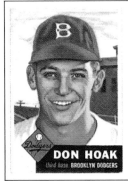

DON HOAK third base BROOKLYN DODGERS

DIXIE HOWELL catcher BROOKLYN DODGERS

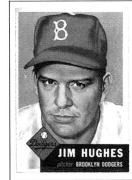

JIM HUGHES pitcher BROOKLYN DODGERS

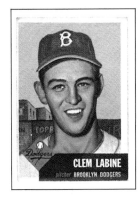

CLEM LABINE pitcher BROOKLYN DODGERS

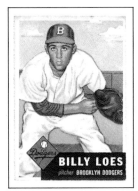

BILLY LOES pitcher BROOKLYN DODGERS

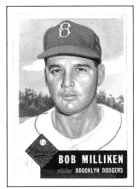

BOB MILLIKEN pitcher BROOKLYN DODGERS

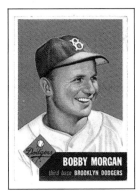

BOBBY MORGAN third base BROOKLYN DODGERS

JOHN PODRES pitcher BROOKLYN DODGERS

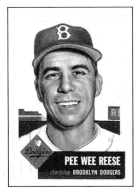

PEE WEE REESE shortstop BROOKLYN DODGERS

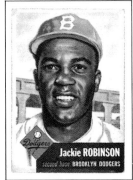

Jackie **ROBINSON** second base BROOKLYN DODGERS

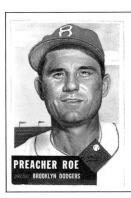

PREACHER ROE pitcher BROOKLYN DODGERS

John RUTHERFORD
pitcher BROOKLYN DODGERS

GEORGE SHUBA
outfielder BROOKLYN DODGERS

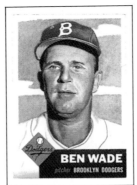

BEN WADE
pitcher BROOKLYN DODGERS

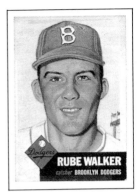

RUBE WALKER
catcher BROOKLYN DODGERS

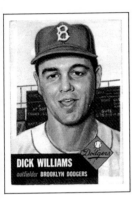

DICK WILLIAMS
outfielder BROOKLYN DODGERS

1954

Walter Alston, a virtual unknown at the major league level, became the Dodgers' skipper in 1954 and no one realized he'd continue to manage the club through the 1976 season. In fact, many believed he wouldn't return for a second season after the Giants downed the Dodgers by five games for the National League flag.

Insufficient pitching and a hand injury to All-Star catcher Roy Campanella were blamed for the Dodgers' demise. Restricted to 111 games, Campanella batted .207 but did hit 19 home runs. Duke Snider, with a .341 average and 40 homers was the club's top producer. Pee Wee Reese swung a .309 stick and Gil Hodges hit .304 with 42 home runs.

Carl Erskine (18-15), Russ Meyer (11-6) and Billy Loes (13-5) were the top pitchers. Don Newcombe, returned from military service, was 9-8. As a staff, the Dodgers posted a lackluster 4.31 ERA, however.

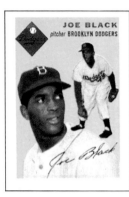

JOE BLACK
pitcher BROOKLYN DODGERS

JUNIOR GILLIAM
second base Brooklyn Dodgers

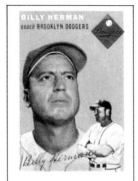

BILLY HERMAN
coach BROOKLYN DODGERS

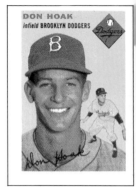

DON HOAK
infield Brooklyn Dodgers

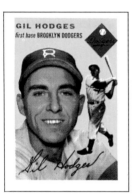

GIL HODGES
first base BROOKLYN DODGERS

JIM HUGHES
pitcher Brooklyn Dodgers

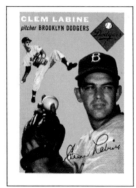

CLEM LABINE
pitcher BROOKLYN DODGERS

TOM LASORDA
pitcher BROOKLYN DODGERS

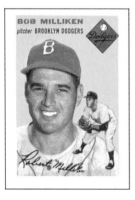

BOB MILLIKEN
pitcher BROOKLYN DODGERS

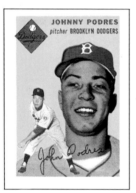

JOHNNY PODRES
pitcher BROOKLYN DODGERS

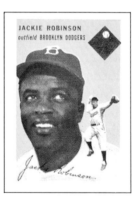

JACKIE ROBINSON
outfield Brooklyn Dodgers

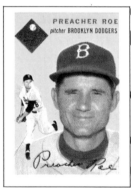

PREACHER ROE
pitcher BROOKLYN DODGERS

DUKE SNIDER
outfield Brooklyn Dodgers

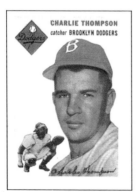

CHARLIE THOMPSON
catcher BROOKLYN DODGERS

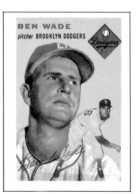

BEN WADE
pitcher BROOKLYN DODGERS

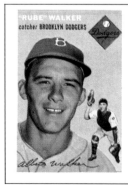

"RUBE" WALKER
catcher BROOKLYN DODGERS

1955

Brooklyn's long-awaited World Series victory became a reality for the Dodgers' long-suffering fans in 1955. The club not only won the pennant by 13½ games but downed the hated Yankees in a seven-game World Series.

The Dodgers won 10 in a row at the outset, 22 of their first two dozen and led by 12½ lengths on July Fourth. Roy Campanella, rebounding from his injury-packed 1954 season, batted .318 with 32 homers and 107 RBIs to win his third MVP award. Carl Furillo batted .314 and Duke Snider .309 while slamming 42 homers and a league-leading 136 RBIs. As a club, the Dodgers hit .271 and socked 201 homers, both tops in the majors.

Pitching was another plus and the staff's 3.68 ERA was the lowest in either league. Don Newcombe, at 20-5, had a 3.19 ERA. Clem Labine, chiefly a reliever, was 13-5. However, Carl Erskine, Billy Loes and Johnny Podres had arm troubles, though the latter won two big games in the Series.

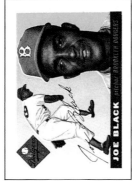
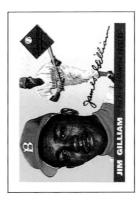

"SANDY" KOUFAX · pitcher · BROOKLYN DODGERS

CLEM LABINE · pitcher · BROOKLYN DODGERS

BOB MILLIKEN · pitcher · BROOKLYN DODGERS

JOHNNY PODRES · pitcher · BROOKLYN DODGERS

JACKIE ROBINSON · BROOKLYN DODGERS

ED ROEBUCK · pitcher · BROOKLYN DODGERS

DUKE SNIDER · outfield · BROOKLYN DODGERS

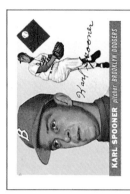

KARL SPOONER · pitcher · BROOKLYN DODGERS

"RUBE" WALKER · catcher · BROOKLYN DODGERS

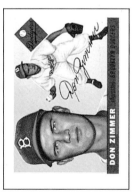

DON ZIMMER · infield · BROOKLYN DODGERS

1956

They couldn't repeat as world champions against the Yankees, but the Dodgers did win a second straight flag in 1956. Unlike the previous season, when they romped to the pennant, Brooklyn didn't clinch until the final day of the season.

Jim Gilliam, at .300, was the club's lone representative in the batters' charmed circle. Duke Snider slugged 41 homers, earning himself the league title, while Gil Hodges had 32 four-baggers and 87 RBIs, three more than Carl Furillo. Roy Campanella, again bothered by hand injuries, hit 20 homers. Jackie Robinson, playing his final season, batted .275 with 10 home runs.

Though Don Newcombe's 27-7 record was the best in the majors, the flag wasn't realized until the late-season addition of Sal Maglie. The veteran righthander was 13-5 including a no-hitter over the Phillies in the season's final week. The staff weakened early when Johnny Podres was inducted into the U.S. Navy.

GIL HODGES
first base BROOKLYN DODGERS

RANDY JACKSON
3rd base BROOKLYN DODGERS

SANDY KOUFAX
pitcher BROOKLYN DODGERS

CLEM LABINE
pitcher BROOKLYN DODGERS

BILLY LOES
pitcher BROOKLYN DODGERS

CHARLEY NEAL
2nd base BROOKLYN DODGERS

DON NEWCOMBE
pitcher BROOKLYN DODGERS

JOHNNY PODRES
pitcher BROOKLYN DODGERS

"PEE WEE" REESE
shortstop BROOKLYN DODGERS

JACKIE ROBINSON
third base BROOKLYN DODGERS

ED ROEBUCK
pitcher BROOKLYN DODGERS

"DUKE" SNIDER
outfield BROOKLYN DODGERS

KARL SPOONER
pitcher BROOKLYN DODGERS

RUBE WALKER
catcher BROOKLYN DODGERS

DON ZIMMER
second base BROOKLYN DODGERS

BROOKLYN DODGERS

1957

The Dodgers' third-place landing in 1957, which severed a string of eight straight seasons in which they finished either first or second, was buried by the stunning October announcement that the club would leave Brooklyn and relocate in Los Angeles in 1958.

Veteran Dodgers began showing their age in the futile attempt to overhaul the flag-winning Braves and only Carl Furillo, at .306, hit over .300. Gil Hodges just missed that figure, but his 98 RBIs paced the team in that regard. Duke Snider hit 40 homers with a .274 batting average.

The pitching left something to be desired. Although Don Drysdale was 17-9 and the returning Johnny Podres had a dozen victories and was the N.L. leader in ERA (2.66) and shutouts (eight), the remainder of the staff couldn't contribute enough. Don Newcombe was 11-12, Roger Craig 6-9, Don Bessent 1-3 and Sal Maglie 6-6.

SANDY AMOROS
BROOKLYN DODGERS OUTFIELD

DON BESSENT
BROOKLYN DODGERS PITCHER

ROY CAMPANELLA
BROOKLYN DODGERS CATCHER

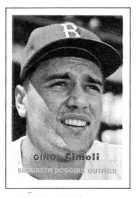
GINO CIMOLI
BROOKLYN DODGERS OUTFIELD

ROGER CRAIG
BROOKLYN DODGERS PITCHER

DON DRYSDALE
BROOKLYN DODGERS PITCHER

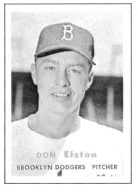
DON ELSTON
BROOKLYN DODGERS PITCHER

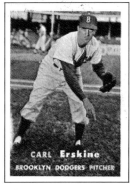
CARL ERSKINE
BROOKLYN DODGERS PITCHER

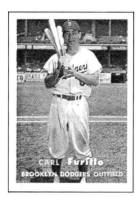

CARL **Furillo**
BROOKLYN DODGERS OUTFIELD

JIM **Gilliam**
BROOKLYN DODGERS 2ndB.—O.F.

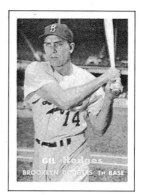

GIL **Hodges**
BROOKLYN DODGERS 1st BASE

RANDY **Jackson**
BROOKLYN DODGERS 3rd BASE

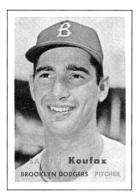

SANDY **Koufax**
BROOKLYN DODGERS PITCHER

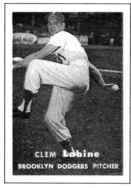

CLEM **Labine**
BROOKLYN DODGERS PITCHER

Labine
BROOKLYN DODGERS PITCHER

SAL **Maglie**
BROOKLYN DODGERS PITCHER

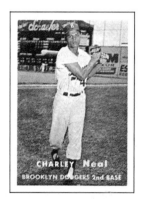

CHARLEY **Neal**
BROOKLYN DODGERS 2nd BASE

DON **Newcombe**
BROOKLYN DODGERS PITCHER

JOHN **Podres**
BROOKLYN DODGERS PITCHER

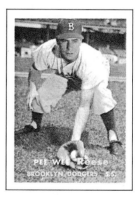

PEE WEE **Reese**
BROOKLYN DODGERS S.S.

DUKE **Snider**
BROOKLYN DODGERS OUTFIELD

Spooner
BROOKLYN DODGERS PITCHER

Walker
BROOKLYN DODGERS CATCHER

DON **Zimmer**
BROOKLYN DODGERS INFIELD

1958

This proved to be a transition year for the Dodgers in many ways. They drew a club-record 1.8 million fans in their first year in Los Angeles, but the adjustment to a new time zone and Memorial Coliseum took its toll in a 71-83 record and seventh-place finish.

Dodger hitters and pitchers had a devilish time in their first season in Los Angeles. Gil Hodges, aided by the Coliseum's short left-field porch, slugged 22 home runs but managed just a .259 average. Duke Snider hit .312 but settled for 15 homers, just six over the distant right-field fence at the Coliseum.

Johnny Podres was the top winner among the Dodger pitchers with a 13-15 record. Don Drysdale was 12-13, Sandy Koufax 11-11, Stan Williams 9-7 and Don Newcombe 0-5 before being traded to Cincinnati.

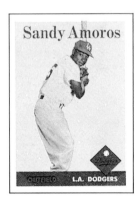

Sandy Amoros

OUTFIELD   L.A. DODGERS

Don Bessent

PITCHER   L. A. DODGERS

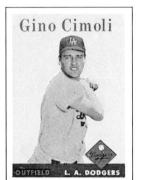

Gino Cimoli

OUTFIELD   L. A. DODGERS

Roger Craig

PITCHER   L. A. DODGERS

Don Demeter

OUTFIELD   L. A. DODGERS

Don Drysdale

PITCHER   L. A. DODGERS

Carl Erskine

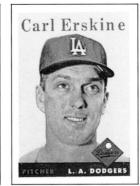

PITCHER   L. A. DODGERS

Carl Furillo

OUTFIELD   L. A. DODGERS

Dick Gray

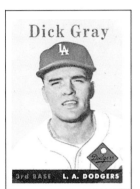

3rd BASE   L. A. DODGERS

Gil Hodges

1st BASE   L. A. DODGERS

Randy Jackson

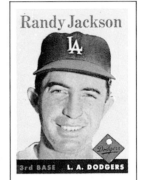

3rd BASE   L. A. DODGERS

Clem Labine

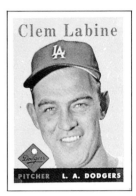

PITCHER   L. A. DODGERS

Danny McDevitt

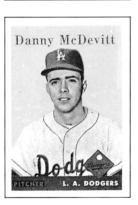

PITCHER   L. A. DODGERS

Charley Neal

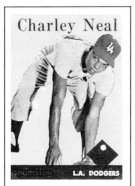

SHORTSTOP   L. A. DODGERS

Don Newcombe

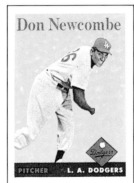

PITCHER   L. A. DODGERS

Joe Pignatano

CATCHER   L. A. DODGERS

Johnny Podres

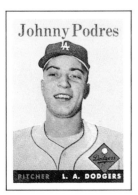

PITCHER   L. A. DODGERS

Pee Wee Reese

S-9-3rd B   L. A. DODGERS

Ed Roebuck

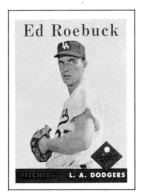

PITCHER   L. A. DODGERS

John Roseboro

CATCHER   L. A. DODGERS

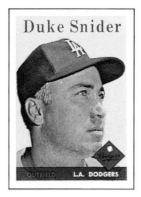

Duke Snider — OUTFIELD — L.A. DODGERS

Elmer Valo — OUTFIELD — L. A. DODGERS

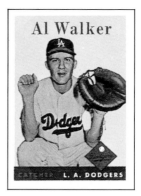

Al Walker — CATCHER — L. A. DODGERS

Don Zimmer — INFIELD — L.A. DODGERS

1959

The phrase "rags to riches" best describes the Dodgers' unprecedented rise from seventh place in 1958 to world champion status in 1959. To achieve their seventh flag in 13 years, the Dodgers had to defeat Milwaukee in a best-of-three playoff for the pennant and then down the White Sox in a six-game World Series.

Wally Moon, acquired from the Cardinals in December 1958, batted .302 and many of his 19 homers were opposite-field shots over the short left-field fence at the Coliseum. Duke Snider, despite knee problems, hit .308 with 23 homers and 88 RBI. Gil Hodges had 25 homers and 80 RBI while Maury Wills, brought up in June, had a hot bat down the stretch that belied his .260 batting average.

Formidable pitching boosted the club, with Don Drysdale's 17 victories high for the staff. Johnny Podres won 14 and Roger Craig, returning from the minors, was 11-5. An emerging Sandy Koufax was 8-6. Larry Sherry, the bullpen king, won seven and saved many more.

jim baxes

LOS ANGELES DODGERS
THIRD BASE

don bessent

LOS ANGELES DODGERS
PITCHER

steve bilko

LOS ANGELES DODGERS
FIRST BASE

SYMBOL OF COURAGE

ROY CAMPANELLA

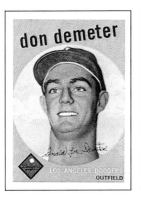

don demeter

LOS ANGELES DODGERS
OUTFIELD

solly drake

LOS ANGELES DODGERS
OUTFIELD

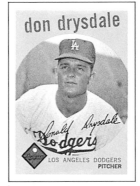

don drysdale

LOS ANGELES DODGERS
PITCHER

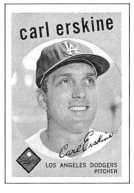

carl erskine

LOS ANGELES DODGERS
PITCHER

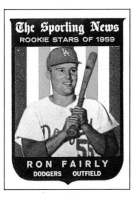

The Sporting News
ROOKIE STARS OF 1959

RON FAIRLY
DODGERS   OUTFIELD

art fowler

LOS ANGELES DODGERS
PITCHER

carl furillo

LOS ANGELES DODGERS
OUTFIELD

bob giallombardo

LOS ANGELES DODGERS
PITCHER

jim gilliam

LOS ANGELES DODGERS
SECOND BASE—OUTFIELD

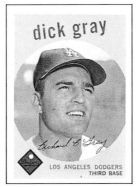

dick gray

LOS ANGELES DODGERS
THIRD BASE

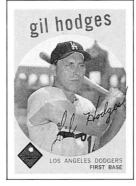

gil hodges

LOS ANGELES DODGERS
FIRST BASE

fred kipp

LOS ANGELES DODGERS
PITCHER

johnny klippstein

LOS ANGELES DODGERS
PITCHER

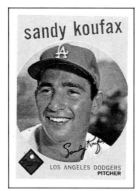

sandy koufax

LOS ANGELES DODGERS
PITCHER

clem labine

LOS ANGELES DODGERS
PITCHER

norm larker

LOS ANGELES DODGERS
FIRST BASE-OUTFIELD

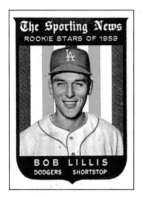

The Sporting News
ROOKIE STARS OF 1959

BOB LILLIS
DODGERS   SHORTSTOP

danny mc devitt

LOS ANGELES DODGERS
PITCHER

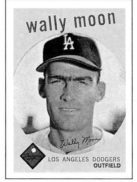

wally moon

LOS ANGELES DODGERS
OUTFIELD

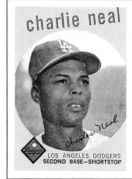

charlie neal

LOS ANGELES DODGERS
SECOND BASE-SHORTSTOP

joe pignatano

LOS ANGELES DODGERS
CATCHER

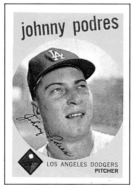

johnny podres

LOS ANGELES DODGERS
PITCHER

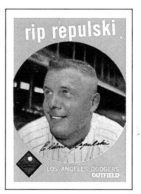

rip repulski

LOS ANGELES DODGERS
OUTFIELD

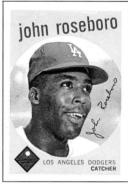

john roseboro

LOS ANGELES DODGERS
CATCHER

duke snider

LOS ANGELES DODGERS
OUTFIELD

gene snyder

LOS ANGELES DODGERS
PITCHER

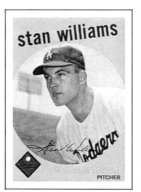

stan williams

LOS ANGELES DODGERS
PITCHER

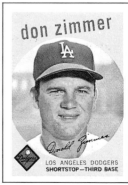

don zimmer

LOS ANGELES DODGERS
SHORTSTOP—THIRD BASE

1960

The Dodgers' see-saw fortunes continued in 1960, when the defending world champions slipped to fourth place. The club made some positive gestures at the midway mark, but from Aug. 1 until the end was never a .500 ballclub.

Norm Larker, at .323, contended for the N.L. batting honors, Wally Moon hit .299 and Maury Wills .295, leading the league with 50 stolen bases. Rookie of the Year Frank Howard banged 23 homers following his arrival from the minors in mid-May.

Don Drysdale's 15 victories was high for the staff. Johnny Podres, Stan Williams and reliever Larry Sherry each won 14. Rodger Craig, out seven weeks with a shoulder ailment, finished 8-3.

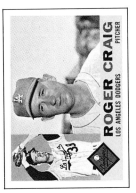

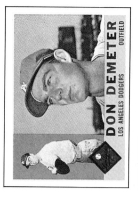

DON DEMETER OUTFIELD
LOS ANGELES DODGERS

DON DRYSDALE PITCHER
LOS ANGELES DODGERS

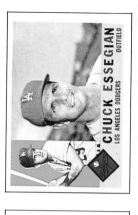

SPORT MAGAZINE '60 ALL-STAR SELECTION
DON DRYSDALE Pitcher (R) National League

CHUCK ESSEGIAN OUTFIELD
LOS ANGELES DODGERS

SELECTED BY THE YOUTH OF AMERICA
RON FAIRLY
LOS ANGELES DODGERS
TOPPS ALL-STAR ROOKIE
OUTFIELD

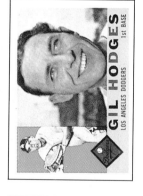

FURILLO BREAKS UP GAME
1959 WORLD SERIES
GAME #3 L.A. 3—SOX 1

CARL FURILLO OUTFIELD
LOS ANGELES DODGERS

JIM GILLIAM THIRD BASE
LOS ANGELES DODGERS

*SPORT MAGAZINE 1960 ROOKIE STAR
BILL HARRIS L.A. DODGERS PITCHER

GIL HODGES 1st BASE
LOS ANGELES DODGERS

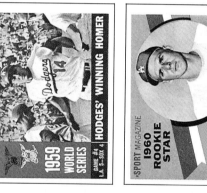

HODGES' WINNING HOMER
1959 WORLD SERIES
GAME #4 L.A. 5—SOX 4

*SPORT MAGAZINE 1960 ROOKIE STAR
FRANK HOWARD L.A. DODGERS 1B-O.F.

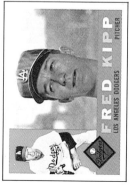

FRED KIPP PITCHER
LOS ANGELES DODGERS

JOHNNY KLIPPSTEIN PITCHER
LOS ANGELES DODGERS

SANDY KOUFAX PITCHER
LOS ANGELES DODGERS

CLEM LABINE PITCHER
LOS ANGELES DODGERS

NORM LARKER — 1st BASE-O.F. — LOS ANGELES DODGERS

BOB LILLIS — SHORTSTOP — LOS ANGELES DODGERS

DANNY McDEVITT — PITCHER — LOS ANGELES DODGERS

WALLY MOON — OUTFIELD — LOS ANGELES DODGERS

CHARLIE NEAL — SECOND BASE — LOS ANGELES DODGERS

1959 WORLD SERIES — GAME #1 — SOX 11 - LA 0 — NEAL STEALS SECOND

1959 WORLD SERIES — GAME #2 — L.A. 4 - SOX 3 — NEAL BELTS 2nd HOMER

SPORT MAGAZINE '60 ALL-STAR SELECTION — CHARLIE NEAL — 2nd Base/National League

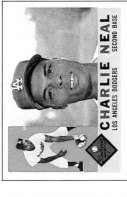

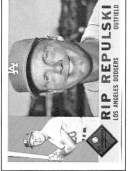

JOE PIGNATANO — CATCHER — LOS ANGELES DODGERS

JOHNNY PODRES — PITCHER — LOS ANGELES DODGERS

ED RAKOW — PITCHER — LOS ANGELES DODGERS

RIP REPULSKI — OUTFIELD — LOS ANGELES DODGERS

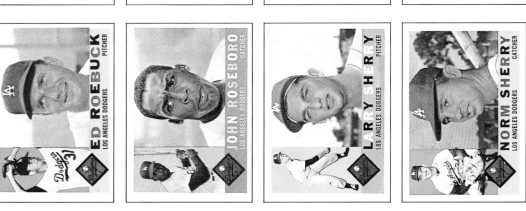

ED ROEBUCK — PITCHER — LOS ANGELES DODGERS

JOHN ROSEBORO — CATCHER — LOS ANGELES DODGERS

LARRY SHERRY — PITCHER — LOS ANGELES DODGERS

NORM SHERRY — CATCHER — LOS ANGELES DODGERS

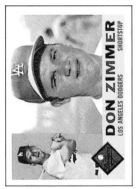

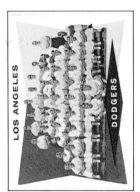

1961

Favored in the pre-season polls to win the National League pennant in 1961, the Dodgers placed second to Cincinnati. A lack of right-handed power in a park where the left-field fence was almost on top of the third baseman hurt the Dodgers' advance.

In August, the club suffered a 10-game losing slide that all but took it out of contention. Lefty-hitting Wally Moon, at .328, led the hitters and newcomer Ron Fairly batted .322. Among the veterans, Gil Hodges hit only .242 and had but eight homers. Duke Snider, despite an elbow ailment, batted .296 with 16 homers.

Sandy Koufax and Johnny Podres, both 18-game winners, plus Don Drysdale's 13 victories gave an indication of the type of pitching that augured well for the Dodgers' future.

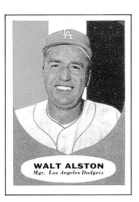

WALT ALSTON
Mgr. Los Angeles Dodgers

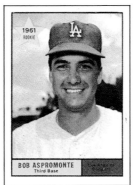

1961 ROOKIE

BOB ASPROMONTE
Third Base
Los Angeles Dodgers

ROGER CRAIG
Pitcher
Los Angeles Dodgers

TOMMY DAVIS
Outfield-Third Base
Los Angeles Dodgers

1961 ROOKIE

WILLIE DAVIS
Outfield
Los Angeles Dodgers

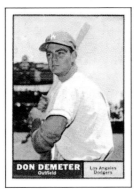

DON DEMETER
Outfield
Los Angeles Dodgers

DON DRYSDALE
Pitcher
Los Angeles Dodgers

RON FAIRLY
Outfield
Los Angeles Dodgers

DICK FARRELL
Pitcher
Los Angeles Dodgers

JIM GILLIAM
Third Base
Los Angeles Dodgers

1961 ROOKIE

JIM GOLDEN
Pitcher
Los Angeles Dodgers

GIL HODGES
First Base-Catcher
Los Angeles Dodgers

FRANK HOWARD
Outfield-First Base
Los Angeles Dodgers

SANDY KOUFAX
Pitcher
Los Angeles Dodgers

NORM LARKER
First Base
Los Angeles Dodgers

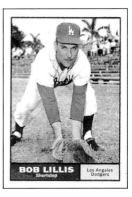

BOB LILLIS
Shortstop
Los Angeles Dodgers

WALLY MOON
Outfield — Los Angeles Dodgers

CHARLIE NEAL
Second Base

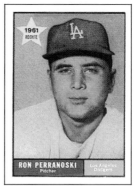

1961 ROOKIE

RON PERRANOSKI
Pitcher — Los Angeles Dodgers

JOE PIGNATANO
Catcher

JOHNNY PODRES
Pitcher — Los Angeles Dodgers

1961 ROOKIE

ED RAKOW
Pitcher — Los Angeles Dodgers

ED ROEBUCK
Pitcher

JOHN ROSEBORO
Catcher — Los Angeles Dodgers

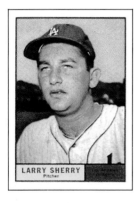

LARRY SHERRY
Pitcher — Los Angeles Dodgers

DUKE SNIDER
Outfield — Los Angeles Dodgers

STAN WILLIAMS
Pitcher — Los Angeles Dodgers

DODGER SOUTHPAWS
(Sandy Koufax-Johnny Podres)

BROTHER BATTERY

LOS ANGELES DODGERS

≡1962

Despite some outstanding individual performances, the season ended in frustration as the Dodgers were overhauled by the Giants, who defeated them in a three-game playoff for the flag. Now housed in brand new Dodger Stadium, the club drew a record 2.7 million. However, when a finger ailment idled Sandy Koufax for more than two months his loss became apparent.

Koufax was 14-7 with a league-leading 2.54 ERA. Don Drysdale, at 25-9, won the Cy Young Award. Johnny Podres finished 15-13 and Stan Williams 14-12.

Tommy Davis, hitting a .342, won the league's batting title. Switch-hitting Maury Wills batted .299 and set a stolen base record with 104, as he captured the MVP award. Big Frank Howard supplied the power, socking 31 homers and driving home 119 runs.

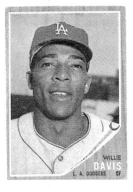

JIM
GILLIAM
L. A. DODGERS 2B-3B

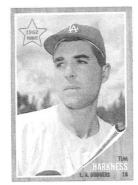

TIM
HARKNESS
L. A. DODGERS 1B

FRANK
HOWARD
L. A. DODGERS 1B-OF

SANDY
KOUFAX
L. A. DODGERS P

WALLY
MOON
L. A. DODGERS OF

PHIL
ORTEGA
L. A. DODGERS P

RON
PERRANOSKI
L. A. DODGERS P

JOHNNY
PODRES
L. A. DODGERS P

PETE
RICHERT
L. A. DODGERS P

ED
ROEBUCK
L. A. DODGERS P

JOHN
ROSEBORO
L. A. DODGERS C

The Sporting News
NATIONAL LEAGUE ALL-STAR

JOHN
ROSEBORO

CATCHER

LARRY
SHERRY
L. A. DODGERS P

NORM
SHERRY
L. A. DODGERS C

DUKE
SNIDER
L. A. DODGERS OF

DARYL
SPENCER
L. A. DODGERS 3B

1963

After the disappointment of 1962, Walter Alston, in his quiet and confident way, pulled a rabbit out of the hat the next season. In addition to winning the flag with a late-season surge, the Dodgers topped it by steamrolling the Yankees in four consecutive games in the World Series.

The pitching of Sandy Koufax and Don Drysdale was formidable. The lefty was 25-5, the ERA leader at 1.88 and the Cy Young recipient. Drysdale finished 19-17 and Johnny Podres 14-12. Lefty reliever Ron Perranoski, 16-3, commanded the bullpen.

Tommy Davis' .326 average again topped the league. Maury Wills hit .302 and led the league with 40 stolen bases. Frank Howard, as usual, provided the longball, clouting a team-high 28 home runs.

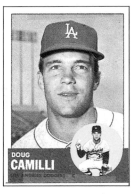

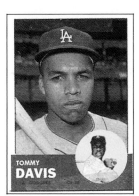

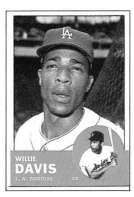

DON
DRYSDALE
DODGERS

RON
FAIRLY
L. A. DODGERS 1B-OF

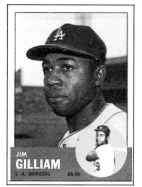

JIM
GILLIAM
L. A. DODGERS 2B-3B

FRANK
HOWARD
L. A. DODGERS OF

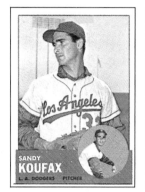

SANDY
KOUFAX
L. A. DODGERS PITCHER

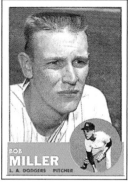

BOB
MILLER
L. A. DODGERS PITCHER

JOE
MOELLER
L. A. DODGERS PITCHER

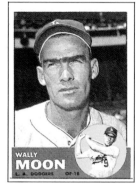

WALLY
MOON
L. A. DODGERS OF-1B

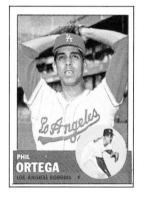

PHIL
ORTEGA
LOS ANGELES DODGERS P

RON
PERRANOSKI
LOS ANGELES DODGERS P

JOHNNY
PODRES
LOS ANGELES DODGERS P

PETE
RICHERT
ANGELES DODGERS P

ED
ROEBUCK
L. A. DODGERS P

JOHN
ROSEBORO
LOS ANGELES DODGERS C

LARRY
SHERRY
L. A. DODGERS PITCHER

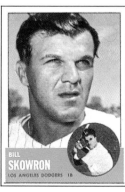

BILL
SKOWRON
LOS ANGELES DODGERS 1B

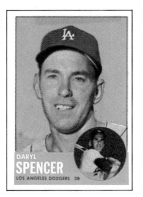

DARYL
SPENCER
LOS ANGELES DODGERS 3B

LEE
WALLS
L. A. DODGERS   OF-1B

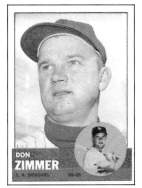

DON
ZIMMER
L. A. DODGERS   3B-2B

DODGERS' BIG THREE
Johnny Podres • Don Drysdale • Sandy Koufax

LOS ANGELES DODGERS

≡1964≡

Offensive and defensive woes and a spate of injuries doomed the Dodgers to sixth place. Tommy Davis, Johnny Podres and Sandy Koufax lost playing time because of injuries.

Podres, who required elbow surgery in June, wound up 0-2. Koufax, despite a league-leading 1.74 ERA and 19-5 record, sat out the final month with an elbow problem. Don Drysdale, 18-16, was a workhorse but couldn't tote the pitching load alone.

Tommy Davis' batting average slumped to .275 and Frank Howard's two dozen homers represented the club's power output. Willie Davis, with 42 stolen bases and a .294 average, began making his presence felt. Maury Wills, with 53 stolen bases, again led the league in that department.

DODGERS

WALT ALSTON   manager

DODGERS

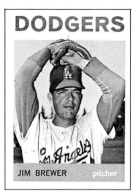

JIM BREWER   pitcher

DODGERS

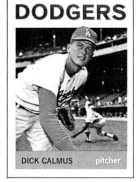

DICK CALMUS   pitcher

DODGERS

DOUG CAMILLI   catcher

DODGERS

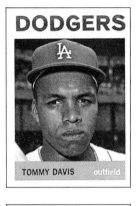

TOMMY DAVIS   outfield

DODGERS

WILLIE DAVIS   outfield

DAVIS SPARKS RALLY

DODGERS

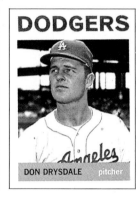

DON DRYSDALE   pitcher

DODGERS

RON FAIRLY   of-1b

DODGERS

JIM GILLIAM   2b-3b

DODGERS

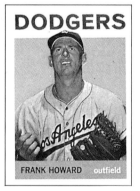

FRANK HOWARD   outfield

KOUFAX STRIKES OUT 15

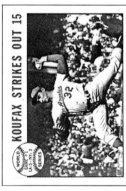

DODGERS

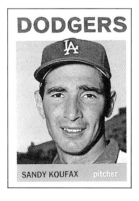

SANDY KOUFAX   pitcher

DODGERS

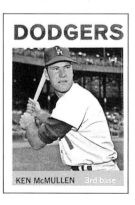

KEN McMULLEN   3rd base

DODGERS

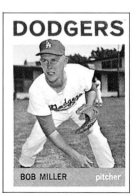

BOB MILLER   pitcher

DODGERS

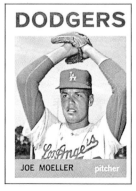

JOE MOELLER   pitcher

DODGERS

WALLY MOON   outfield

DODGERS

PHIL ORTEGA   pitcher

DODGERS

RON PERRANOSKI   pitcher

DODGERS

JOHNNY PODRES   pitcher

DODGERS

PETE RICHERT   pitcher

DODGERS

JOHN ROSEBORO   catcher

DODGERS

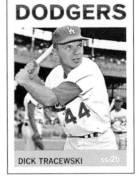

DICK TRACEWSKI   ss-2b

DODGERS

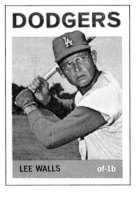

LEE WALLS   of-1b

1964 ROOKIE STARS
DODGERS

AL FERRARA   OUTFIELD

JEFF TORBORG   CATCHER

1964 ROOKIE STARS
DODGERS

DICK NEN   FIRST BASE

NICK WILLHITE   PITCHER

1964 ROOKIE STARS
DODGERS

WES PARKER   1st B-OF

JOHN WERHAS   3rd BASE

L. A. DODGERS

L. A. TAKES 3RD STRAIGHT

SEALING YANKS' DOOM

THE DODGERS CELEBRATE

1965

The Dodgers, enjoying another of their "put it all together" seasons, regained the heights in 1965, winning the National League pennant by two games and then defeating Minnesota in a seven-game World Series.

It was a success built strictly on pitching, solid defense and the .286 batting average and 96 stolen bases of Maury Wills. As a club, the Dodgers hit only .245 and collected a mere 78 homers, fewest in the majors.

Sandy Koufax, the unanimous Cy Young selection, had his fourth no-hitter in as many years — this one a perfect game over the Cubs. The left-hander was 26-8 and the ERA leader at 2.04. Fellow southpaw Claude Osteen was 15-5, while Don Drysdale won 23 and lost 12.

A fractured right ankle on May 1 idled Tommy Davis. Four days later a broken finger sidelined Al Ferrara, an injury that promoted Lou Johnson from the minors. Johnson, batting .259, hit a dozen homers and provided a spark to the Dodgers' sputtering offense. He also was hero of the World Series.

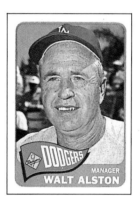
MANAGER
WALT ALSTON

PITCHER
JIM BREWER

CATCHER
DOUG CAMILLI

OUTFIELD
TOMMY DAVIS

OUTFIELD
WILLIE DAVIS

PITCHER
DON DRYSDALE

1B-OUTFIELD
RON FAIRLY

OUTFIELD
DERRELL GRIFFITH

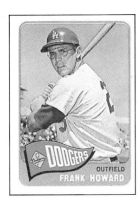

DODGERS
OUTFIELD
FRANK HOWARD

DODGERS
3 B-SHORTSTOP
JOHN KENNEDY

DODGERS
PITCHER
SANDY KOUFAX

DODGERS
PITCHER
BOB MILLER

DODGERS
PITCHER
JOE MOELLER

DODGERS
OUTFIELD
WALLY MOON

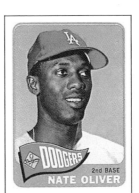

DODGERS
2nd BASE
NATE OLIVER

DODGERS
PITCHER
CLAUDE OSTEEN

DODGERS
OF-1st BASE
WES PARKER

DODGERS
PITCHER
RON PERRANOSKI

DODGERS
PITCHER
JOHNNY PODRES

DODGERS
PITCHER
HOWIE REED

DODGERS
CATCHER
JOHN ROSEBORO

DODGERS
OF-1B
DICK SMITH

DODGERS
CATCHER
JEFF TORBORG

DODGERS
2B-SS
DICK TRACEWSKI

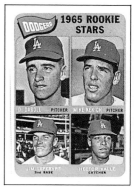

1966

The Dodgers, linking National League flags for the first time since Milwaukee did it in 1957-58, had their 1966 season dimmed somewhat by a World Series sweep at the hands of the Baltimore Orioles.

Not one of the league's power clubs, the Dodgers had to scramble from the outset and finally defeated the Giants by a game and a half on the season's final day. Again it was pitching and defense that won Walter Alston his sixth flag in 13 years at the Dodgers' helm.

The staff pitched to a 2.62 ERA, the slimmest in the N.L. in 23 years. Sandy Koufax, in his final season, ignored his arthritic elbow to win 27 and claim his second unanimous Cy Young Award in as many seasons. His 1.73 ERA enabled him to lead the league for the fifth consecutive season. Don Drysdale (13-16), Claude Osteen (17-14) and Don Sutton (12-12) complemented Koufax. Ron Perranoski and Phil Regan were the big bulls in the 'pen.

Jim Lefebvre's 24 homers led the club, while the rebounding Tommy Davis hit .313. Willie Davis finished at .284 and Lou Johnson at .272.

WALT ALSTON manager

JIM BREWER pitcher

TOMMY DAVIS outfield

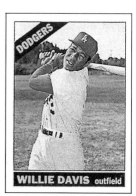

WILLIE DAVIS outfield

DON DRYSDALE   pitcher

RON FAIRLY   outfield

AL FERRARA   outfield

DERRELL GRIFFITH   outfield

LOU JOHNSON   outfield

JOHN KENNEDY   3rd base

SANDY KOUFAX   pitcher

JIM LEFEBVRE   2nd base

DON LE JOHN   3rd base

BOB MILLER   pitcher

JOE MOELLER   pitcher

NATE OLIVER   2nd base

CLAUDE OSTEEN   pitcher

WES PARKER   1b-of

RON PERRANOSKI   pitcher

JOHNNY PODRES   pitcher

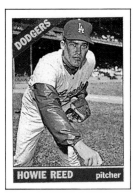

HOWIE REED   pitcher

PHIL REGAN   pitcher

JOHN ROSEBORO   catcher

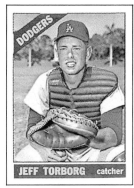

JEFF TORBORG   catcher

HECTOR VALLE   catcher

NICK WILLHITE   pitcher

DODGERS   1ST PLACE NATIONAL LEAGUE

1966 ROOKIE STARS   DON SUTTON   BILL SINGER   DODGERS

1967

Sandy Koufax's retirement signaled the beginning of a new era, and injuries plus some of their key people having "off" seasons, contributed to the Dodgers' eighth-place finish.

Jim Lefebvre, Rod Fairly, Wes Parker and Willie Davis didn't contribute as previously, although John Roseboro and newcomer Al Ferrara did. The latter hit .277 with 16 homers, while Roseboro batted .272.

Right-hander Bill Singer, 12-8 with a 2.65 ERA, was the Dodgers' top pitcher. Despite a rosy 2.74 earned run average, Don Drysdale was 13-16, Claude Osteen 17-17 and Don Sutton 11-15.

WALT ALSTON • MANAGER

DODGERS

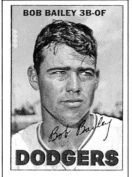

BOB BAILEY 3B-OF

DODGERS

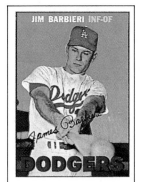

JIM BARBIERI INF-OF

DODGERS

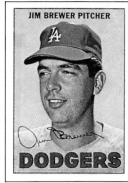

JIM BREWER PITCHER

DODGERS

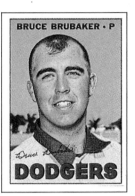

BRUCE BRUBAKER • P

DODGERS

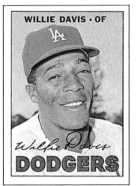

WILLIE DAVIS • OF

DODGERS

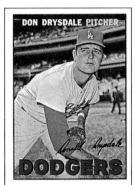

DON DRYSDALE PITCHER

DODGERS

DICK EGAN • PITCHER

DODGERS

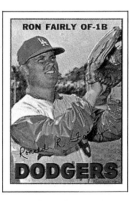

RON FAIRLY OF-1B

DODGERS

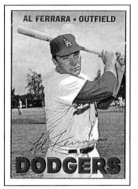

AL FERRARA • OUTFIELD

DODGERS

JIM HICKMAN • OF

DODGERS

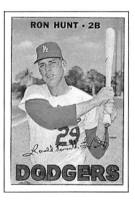

RON HUNT • 2B

DODGERS

LOU JOHNSON • OUTFIELD

DODGERS

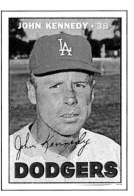

JOHN KENNEDY • 3B

DODGERS

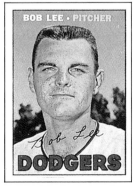

BOB LEE • PITCHER

DODGERS

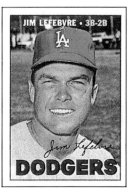

JIM LEFEBVRE • 3B-2B

DODGERS

BOB MILLER · PITCHER

DODGERS

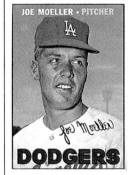

JOE MOELLER · PITCHER

DODGERS

CLAUDE OSTEEN · P

DODGERS

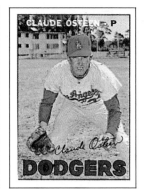

WES PARKER · 1B-OF

DODGERS

RON PERRANOSKI · P

DODGERS

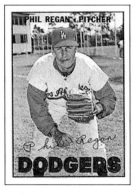

PHIL REGAN · PITCHER

DODGERS

JOHN ROSEBORO · C

DODGERS

DICK SCHOFIELD · 3B-SS

DODGERS

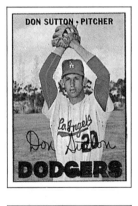

DON SUTTON · PITCHER

DODGERS

JEFF TORBORG · CATCHER

DODGERS

JOHN WERHAS · INFIELD

DODGERS

DODGERS

DODGERS 1967 ROOKIE STARS

BILL SINGER P

J. CAMPANIS C

DODGERS 1967 ROOKIE STARS

GENE MICHAEL · SS

TOM HUTTON · 1B

≡1968≡

Lack of power short-circuited the Dodgers' 1968 efforts and the club placed seventh, 21 lengths behind the flag-winning Cardinals.

As a unit, the Dodgers batted a mere .230 and hit but 68 home runs. Catcher Tom Haller, acquired from the Giants, was the top batsman at .285. Willie Crawford, a bonus-boy outfielder, hit .251 in 61 games.

The pitching, primarily the work of Don Drysdale, was superb. Big D., 14-12, had a 2.15 ERA. In May and June he established a shutout record when he hurled 56.2 consecutive scoreless innings. Don Sutton finished 11-15 and lefty Claude Osteen 11-18.

HANK AGUIRRE

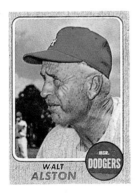
WALT ALSTON

BOB BAILEY

JIM BREWER

JIM CAMPANIS

WILLIE CRAWFORD

WILLIE DAVIS

DON DRYSDALE

RON **FAIRLY**
OUTFIELD DODGERS

AL **FERRARA**
OUTFIELD DODGERS

LEN **GABRIELSON**
OUTFIELD DODGERS

JIM **GRANT**
PITCHER DODGERS

RON **HUNT**
2nd BASE DODGERS

JIM **LEFEBVRE**
3B-2B DODGERS

NATE **OLIVER**
2B-SS DODGERS

CLAUDE **OSTEEN**
PITCHER DODGERS

WES **PARKER**
1st BASE DODGERS

PAUL **POPOVICH**
INFIELD DODGERS

JOHN **PURDIN**
PITCHER DODGERS

PHIL **REGAN**
PITCHER DODGERS

JOHN **ROSEBORO**
CATCHER DODGERS

BILL **SINGER**
PITCHER DODGERS

DON **SUTTON**
PITCHER DODGERS

JEFF **TORBORG**
CATCHER DODGERS

1969

It was the year they split the league into two divisions and the best the Dodgers could do was a fourth-place finish in the six-team Western Division of the National League. Actually, Walter Alston had his club in contention for much of the race until slipping in September.

Outfielder Andy Kosco paced the club in homers (19) and RBI (74) while Maury Wills, returning in a deal with Montreal, batted .297. Manny Mota, who accompanied Wills back to Los Angeles, batted .323 in 85 games. Wes Parker hit .278 and infielder Ted Sizemore earned Rookie of the Year honors with his .271 average.

The pitching was a plus again, despite the retirement of Don Drysdale in August. The tall right-hander was 5-4 when he called it a career. Bill Singer, 20-12, and Claude Osteen, 20-15, led the staff. Don Sutton finished with a 17-18 log.

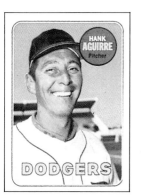

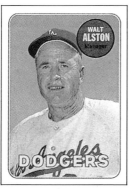

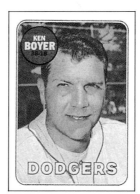

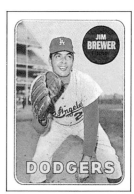

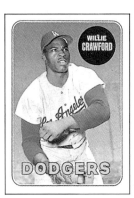

WILLIE CRAWFORD
Outfield

DODGERS

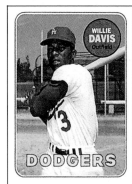

WILLIE DAVIS
Outfield

DODGERS

DON DRYSDALE
Pitcher

DODGERS

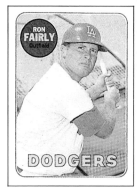

RON FAIRLY
Outfield

DODGERS

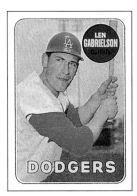

LEN GABRIELSON
Outfield

DODGERS

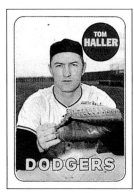

TOM HALLER
Catcher

DODGERS

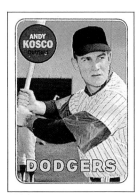

ANDY KOSCO
Outfield

DODGERS

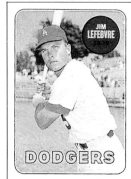

JIM LEFEBVRE
2B-3B

DODGERS

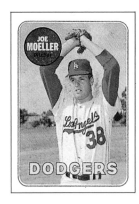

JOE MOELLER
Pitcher

DODGERS

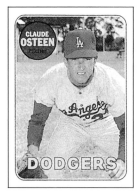

CLAUDE OSTEEN
Pitcher

DODGERS

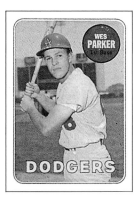

WES PARKER
1B-Outfield

DODGERS

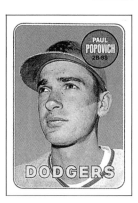

PAUL POPOVICH
2B-SS

DODGERS

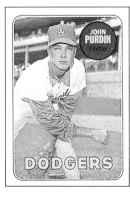

JOHN PURDIN
Pitcher

DODGERS

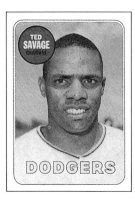

TED SAVAGE
Outfield

DODGERS

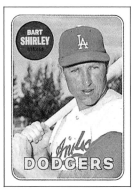

BART SHIRLEY
Infield

DODGERS

BILL SINGER
Pitcher

DODGERS

 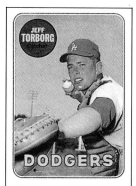 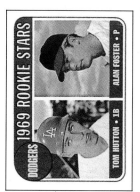 

1970

The Dodgers' long-slumbering bats began making some noise in 1970, but their efforts couldn't match Cincinnati's Big Red Machine, whose 102 wins dominated the National League. The Dodgers finished second in the Western Division, 14½ games behind the vaunted Reds.

Wes Parker paced the club with a .319 average and 111 RBI. Ted Sizemore hit .306, and with Willie Davis and Manny Mota at .305, the club had a quartet over .300.

The pitchers sagged, however. Don Sutton was 15-13, and despite a no-hitter vs Philadelphia, Bill Singer, bothered by injuries, finished 8-5. Alan Foster was 10-13.

Walter Alston | MANAGER

Jim Brewer | PITCHER

Willie Crawford | OUTFIELD

Willie Davis | OUTFIELD

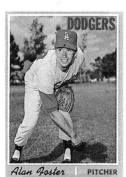
Alan Foster | PITCHER

Len Gabrielson | OUTFIELD

B. Grabarkewitz | INFIELD

Tom Haller | CATCHER

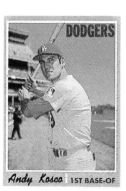
Andy Kosco | 1ST BASE-OF

Jim Lefebvre | 2B-3B

Al McBean | PITCHER

Joe Moeller | PITCHER

Manny Mota | OUTFIELD

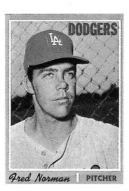
Fred Norman | PITCHER

Claude Osteen | PITCHER

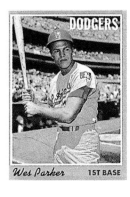
Wes Parker | 1ST BASE

Jose Pena | PITCHER

Bill Russell | OUTFIELD

Bill Singer | PITCHER

Ted Sizemore | 2ND BASE

Bill Sudakis | 3RD BASE

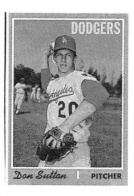

Don Sutton | PITCHER

Jeff Torborg | CATCHER

Maury Wills SHORTSTOP

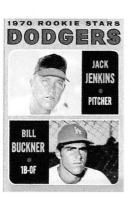

1970 ROOKIE STARS
DODGERS

JACK JENKINS PITCHER

BILL BUCKNER 1B-OF

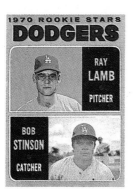

1970 ROOKIE STARS
DODGERS

RAY LAMB PITCHER

BOB STINSON CATCHER

LOS ANGELES DODGERS

≡1971≡

In one of their finest efforts in years, a re-made Dodgers' roster, in the race all the way, finished second, one game behind the division-winning Giants.

Willie Davis batted .309 and Dick Allen .295 with 23 homers and 90 RBI. Willie Crawford chipped in with a .287 average and the seemingly ageless Maury Wills hit .281. Manny Mota, in 91 appearances, ended at .312.

The pitching, particularly that of left-hander Al Downing, made a difference. Downing, acquired from Milwaukee, responded with a 20-9 season and a 2.68 ERA. Don Sutton ended 17-12 and Claude Osteen 14-11. Bill Singer was 10-17.

DODGERS		DODGERS		DODGERS		DODGERS	
rich allen •	outfield	walt alston •	manager	jim brewer •	pitcher	willie crawford •	outfield

 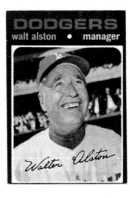 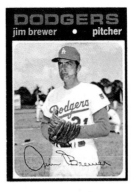 

DODGERS		DODGERS		DODGERS		DODGERS	
willie davis •	outfield	alan foster •	pitcher	steve garvey •	3rd base	billy grabarkewitz •	3b

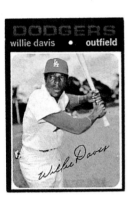 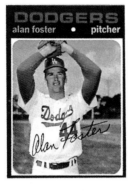 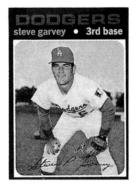 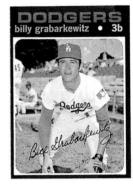

DODGERS		DODGERS		DODGERS		DODGERS	
tom haller •	catcher	von joshua •	outfield	jim lefebvre •	2b-3b	joe moeller •	pitcher

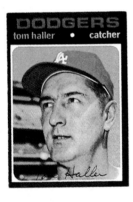   

DODGERS		DODGERS		DODGERS		DODGERS	
manny mota •	outfield	claude osteen •	pitcher	wes parker •	1st base	jose pena •	pitcher

   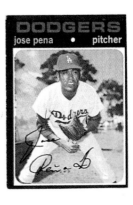

bill russell • outfield

bill singer • pitcher

jerry stephenson • pitcher

bill sudakis • 3b-catcher

don sutton • pitcher

jeff torborg • catcher

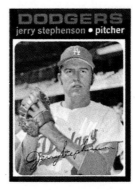

sandy vance • pitcher

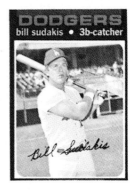

maury wills • shortstop

1971 ROOKIE STARS
DODGERS

bob valentine • shortstop

mike strahler • pitcher

DODGERS

1972

The Dodgers, favored to win the National League West, managed just a third-place finish.

Divisional leaders into June, when a defensive break-down caused them to stumble badly, the club did get profitable seasons from several hitters. Manny Mota hit .323 and Bill Buckner .319. Willie Davis hit .289 with 19 homers and Steve Garvey .269. Injury-plagued Frank Robinson hit .251 with 19 home runs.

Don Sutton, 19-9, led the moundsmen with a 2.08 ERA. Claude Osteen was 20-11 and 2.64 and Tommy John, obtained from the White Sox, was 11-5 and 2.89. Al Downing finished at 9-9. Bill Singer, in his final Dodger season, was 6-16 though pitching to a 3.67 earned run average.

WALTER ALSTON

JIM BREWER

BILL BUCKNER

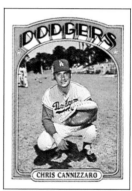
CHRIS CANNIZZARO

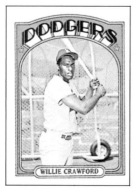
WILLIE CRAWFORD

WILLIE DAVIS

AL DOWNING

JOE FERGUSON

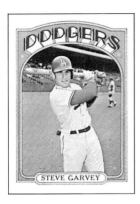

STEVE GARVEY

BILLY GRABARKEWITZ

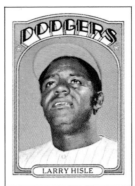

LARRY HISLE

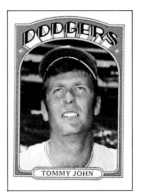

TOMMY JOHN

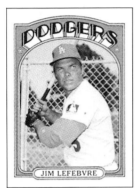

JIM LEFEBVRE

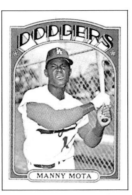

MANNY MOTA

CLAUDE OSTEEN

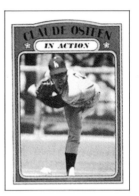

CLAUDE OSTEEN
IN ACTION

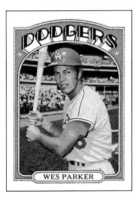

WES PARKER

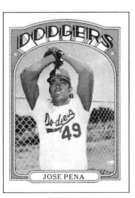

JOSE PENA

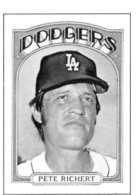

PETE RICHERT

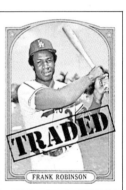

FRANK ROBINSON

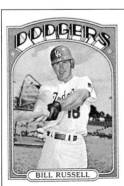

BILL RUSSELL

DUKE SIMS

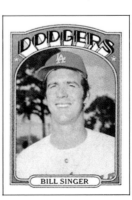

BILL SINGER

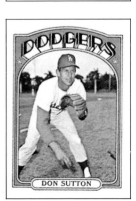

DON SUTTON

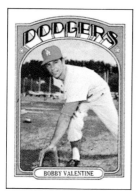

BOBBY VALENTINE

HOYT WILHELM

MAURY WILLS

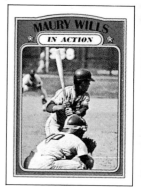

MAURY WILLS IN ACTION

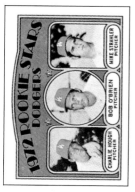

1972 ROOKIE STARS DODGERS — MIKE STRAHLER PITCHER / BOB O'BRIEN PITCHER / CHARLIE HOUGH PITCHER

DODGERS

1973

A blend of youth and experience was the Dodgers story in 1973. The club, which led for most of the race, landed second, three and a half lengths behind Cincinnati.

Rookies Davey Lopes and Ron Cey contributed nicely and Steve Garvey hit .304 and drove in 50 runners. Veteran Willie Davis batted .285 with 16 homers and 77 runs batted in and shortstop Bill Russell, improved defensively, added a .265 batting average. Willie Crawford hit .295 with 14 homers and 66 RBI.

The staff led the league with a 3.00 earned run average and a quartet won 14 or more. Don Sutton went 18-10, Tommy John 16-7 and Claude Osteen 16-11. Andy Messersmith was 14-10 and Al Downing 9-9. Jim Brewer, with 20 saves, was the ace out of the Dodgers' bullpen.

COACHES
RED ADAMS
JIM GILLIAM
MONTY BASGALL
TOM LASORDA

WALT ALSTON
L. A. DODGERS
MANAGER

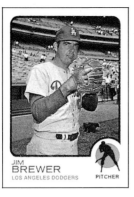

JIM BREWER
LOS ANGELES DODGERS
PITCHER

BILL BUCKNER
LOS ANGELES DODGERS
1st BASE

WILLIE CRAWFORD
LOS ANGELES DODGERS
OUTFIELD

WILLIE DAVIS
LOS ANGELES DODGERS
OUTFIELD

DICK DIETZ
LOS ANGELES DODGERS
CATCHER

AL DOWNING
LOS ANGELES DODGERS
PITCHER

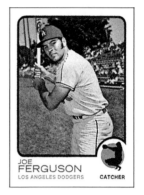

JOE FERGUSON
LOS ANGELES DODGERS
CATCHER

STEVE GARVEY
LOS ANGELES DODGERS
3rd BASE

TOMMY JOHN
LOS ANGELES DODGERS
PITCHER

VON JOSHUA
LOS ANGELES DODGERS
OUTFIELD

LEE LACY
LOS ANGELES DODGERS
2nd BASE

KEN McMULLEN
LOS ANGELES DODGERS
3rd BASE

ANDY MESSERSMITH
LOS ANGELES DODGERS
PITCHER

MANNY MOTA
LOS ANGELES DODGERS
OUTFIELD

CLAUDE OSTEEN
LOS ANGELES DODGERS
PITCHER

WES PARKER
LOS ANGELES DODGERS
1st BASE

PETE
RICHERT
LOS ANGELES DODGERS   PITCHER

BILL
RUSSELL
LOS ANGELES DODGERS   SHORTSTOP

DON
SUTTON
LOS ANGELES DODGERS   PITCHER

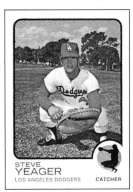

STEVE
YEAGER
LOS ANGELES DODGERS   CATCHER

LOS ANGELES DODGERS

1974

An eight-year journey to the top ended in 1974 when the Dodgers finally outlasted the persistent Reds to win the Western Division by four games.

Center-fielder Jim Wynn and reliever Mike Marshall made the difference. Wynn batted .271, popped 32 homers and drove in 108 runs. Marshall, appearing in a record 106 games, won 15, saved 21 and pitched to a 2.42 ERA in winning the Cy Young Award.

Assisting Wynn on the attack were MVP Steve Garvey (.312), Bill Buckner (.314), Willie Crawford (.295) and Steve Yeager (.266). Despite losing Tommy John, a 13-game winner when his arm blew out in July, the Dodgers received excellent hurling from Andy Messersmith (20-6), Don Sutton (19-9), Charlie Hough (9-4), Doug Rau (13-11) and the almost peerless Marshall from the 'pen. The long blot came in the World Series, when the Dodgers bowed in five games to the Oakland A's.

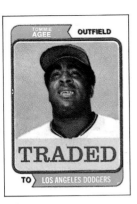

TOMMIE AGEE OUTFIELD

TRADED

TO LOS ANGELES DODGERS

LOS ANGELES MANAGER

COACHES

Tom Lasorda · Jim Gilliam · Red Adams · Monty Basgall

WALTER ALSTON DODGERS

LOS ANGELES SHORTSTOP

RICK AUERBACH DODGERS

LOS ANGELES PITCHER

JIM BREWER DODGERS

LOS ANGELES 1st BASE

BILL BUCKNER DODGERS

LOS ANGELES 3rd BASE

RON CEY DODGERS

LOS ANGELES OUTFIELD

WILLIE CRAWFORD DODGERS

LOS ANGELES OUTFIELD

WILLIE DAVIS DODGERS

LOS ANGELES PITCHER

AL DOWNING DODGERS

C LOS ANGELES DODGERS

JOE FERGUSON

STEVE GARVEY 3B-1B LOS ANGELES DODGERS

LOS ANGELES PITCHER

CHARLIE HOUGH DODGERS

LOS ANGELES PITCHER

TOMMY JOHN DODGERS

LOS ANGELES OUTFIELD

VON JOSHUA DODGERS

LOS ANGELES 2nd BASE

LEE LACY DODGERS

LOS ANGELES 2nd BASE

DAVE LOPES DODGERS

MIKE MARSHALL — PITCHER
TRADED TO LOS ANGELES DODGERS

LOS ANGELES — 3rd BASE
KEN McMULLEN — DODGERS

LOS ANGELES — PITCHER
ANDY MESSERSMITH — DODGERS

LOS ANGELES — OUTFIELD
MANNY MOTA — DODGERS

LOS ANGELES — PITCHER
CLAUDE OSTEEN — DODGERS

LOS ANGELES — OUTFIELD
TOM PACIOREK — DODGERS

LOS ANGELES — PITCHER
DOUG RAU — DODGERS

LOS ANGELES — PITCHER
PETE RICHERT — DODGERS

LOS ANGELES — SHORTSTOP
BILL RUSSELL — DODGERS

LOS ANGELES — PITCHER
DON SUTTON — DODGERS

LOS ANGELES — CATCHER
STEVE YEAGER — DODGERS

LOS ANGELES DODGERS

≡ 1975 ≡

Injuries, sub-par Dodger performances and the superiority of the Reds resulted in Cincinnati besting the second-place Dodgers by 20 games.

Bill Russell, Bill Buckner and Joe Ferguson were among the injured, while Steve Garvey, Ron Cey and Davey Lopes were among the healthy. Garvey batted .319 and Lopes led the league with 77 stolen bases. Cey slammed 25 homers and had 101 runs batted in.

Dodgers pitchers posted a 2.92 ERA, with Andy Messersmith winning 19 games. Burt Hooton won 18, Don Sutton 16 and Doug Rau 15. Mike Marshall, still the big man in the bullpen, won nine and saved 13.

RICK AUERBACH

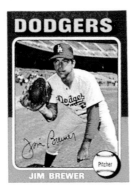
JIM BREWER

BILL BUCKNER

RON CEY

AL DOWNING

JOE FERGUSON

STEVE GARVEY

DODGERS

CHARLIE HOUGH

Pitcher

DODGERS

TOMMY JOHN

Pitcher

DODGERS

VON JOSHUA

Outfield

DODGERS

LEE LACY

2nd Base

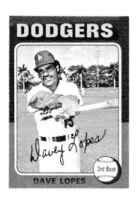

DODGERS

DAVE LOPES

2nd Base

'74 Highlights

MARSHALL HURLS IN 106 GAMES

DODGERS

MIKE MARSHALL

Pitcher

DODGERS

KEN McMULLEN

3rd Base

DODGERS

ANDY MESSERSMITH

NL
ALL STAR
Pitcher

DODGERS

MANNY MOTA

Outfield

DODGERS

TOM PACIOREK

Outfield

DODGERS

DOUG RAU

Pitcher

DODGERS

BILL RUSSELL

Shortstop

DODGERS

DON SUTTON

Pitcher

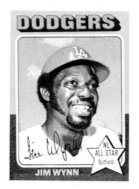

DODGERS

JIM WYNN

NL
ALL STAR
Outfield

DODGERS

STEVE YEAGER

Catcher

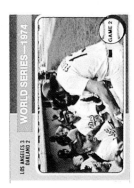

≡1976

Second best to Cincinnati, this time by 10 games in arrears, was the Dodgers' story. Walter Alston retired after 23 seasons as the ballclub's skipper.

Steve Garvey, at .317, led the offense and his 80 RBI were matched by third baseman Ron Cey. Dusty Baker, obtained from Atlanta, finished with just four homers and a .242 batting average. Bill Buckner hit .301 and Manny Mota .281. Reggie Smith, acquired from the Cardinals, batted .280 with 10 homers. Davey Lopes, nursing injuries, led the league with 66 stolen bases.

Among the pitchers, Don Sutton was 21-10 and Tommy John, after missing a season and a half with an arm ailment, finished 10-10. Rick Rhoden posted a 12-3 mark and Doug Rau won 16 games with a nifty 2.57 ERA. Mike Marshall was traded to Atlanta and knuckle-baller Charlie Hough replaced him in the 'pen with a dozen wins and 18 saves.

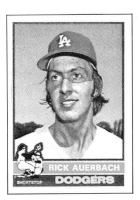

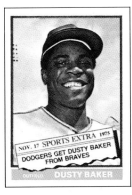

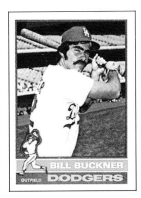

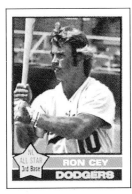

WILLIE CRAWFORD
OUTFIELD DODGERS

AL DOWNING
PITCHER DODGERS

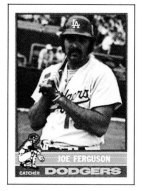

JOE FERGUSON
CATCHER DODGERS

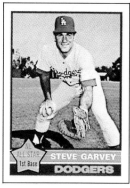

ALL STAR 1st Base
STEVE GARVEY
DODGERS

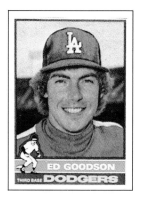

ED GOODSON
THIRD BASE DODGERS

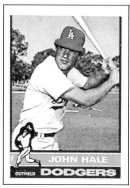

JOHN HALE
OUTFIELD DODGERS

BURT HOOTON
PITCHER DODGERS

CHARLIE HOUGH
PITCHER DODGERS

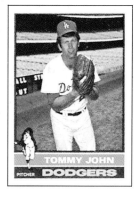

TOMMY JOHN
PITCHER DODGERS

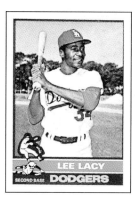

LEE LACY
SECOND BASE DODGERS

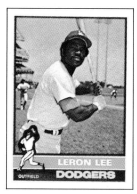

LERON LEE
OUTFIELD DODGERS

'75 RECORD BREAKER
DAVE LOPES
LOS ANGELES DODGERS

★ MOST CONSECUTIVE SUCCESSFUL
STOLEN BASE ATTEMPTS—38

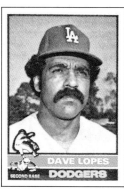

DAVE LOPES
SECOND BASE DODGERS

MIKE MARSHALL
PITCHER DODGERS

KEN McMULLEN
THIRD BASE DODGERS

ANDY MESSERSMITH
PITCHER DODGERS

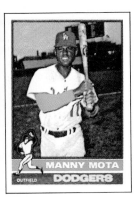

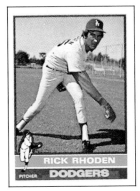

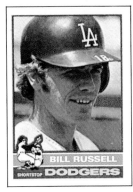

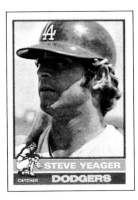

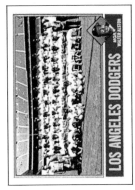

1977

Tommy Lasorda's first season as the Dodgers' manager ushered in a new golden era for the Dodgers, who won the pennant, but lost in six games to the Yankees in the World Series.

An advocate of getting out of the gate fast, Lasorda got his wish as his hustling club won 17 of its first 20 games and never looked back, winning the Western Division by 10 games.

In addition to the usual quality pitching, the Dodgers hit 191 home runs, including 30 or more from a quartet of Steve Garvey (33), Reggie Smith (32), Ron Cey (30) and Dusty Baker (30).

Tommy John's 20-7 record and 2.78 ERA paced the pitching staff. Rick Rhoden won 16 and Doug Rau 14, after winning 11 of his first 12 decisions. Don Sutton won 14 and Burt Hooton 12. Charlie Hough, working from the bullpen, had 19 saves and Mike Garman a dozen.

DODGERS
DUSTY BAKER — OUTFIELD
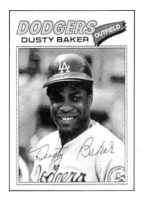

DODGERS
BILL BUCKNER — OF-1B
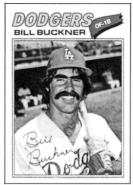

DODGERS
RON CEY — 3rd BASE

DODGERS
STEVE GARVEY — 1st BASE
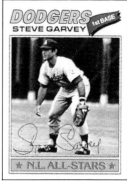
★ N.L. ALL-STARS ★

DODGERS
ED GOODSON — 3B-1B
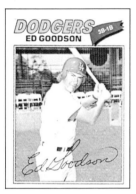

DODGERS
JOHN HALE — OUTFIELD

DODGERS
BURT HOOTON — PITCHER

DODGERS
CHARLIE HOUGH — PITCHER

DODGERS
TOMMY JOHN — PITCHER
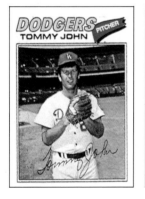

DODGERS
LEE LACY — 2B-OF

DODGERS
DAVE LOPES — 2nd BASE
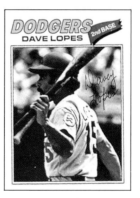

DODGERS
MANNY MOTA — OUTFIELD

DODGERS
DOUG RAU — PITCHER

DODGERS
RICK RHODEN — PITCHER
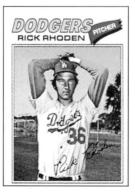

DODGERS
ELLIE RODRIGUEZ — CATCHER
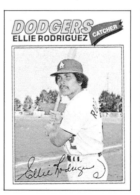

DODGERS
BILL RUSSELL — SHORTSTOP
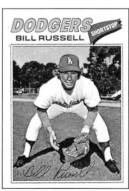

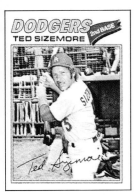

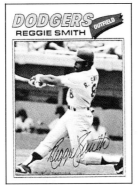

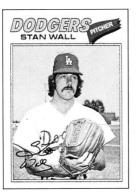

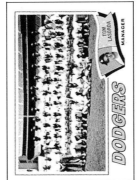

1978

The Dodgers made it two-for-two when they repeated as National League champions, but their fall frustration continued, as they again fell to the Yankees in six games.

Unlike 1977, when the longball was so evident and four of the Dodgers hit 30 or more homers, the 1978 edition didn't have one player reach that figure. Reggie Smith, with 29, was the club leader. Steve Garvey batted .316, while Davey Lopes hit .278 with 17 homers and stole 45 of 49 bases. Ron Cey slugged 23 homers and had 84 RBI.

Pitching was the club's strong point, the hurlers leading the league with a composite 3.12 ERA. Burt Hooton was the big winner with 19 and Tommy John went 17-10, being slowed down the stretch by a leg ailment. The bullpen, led by free agent Terry Forster, also produced. Forster had 22 saves, eight in the final month as the Dodgers became the first club in major league history to draw three million in home attendance.

Dodgers — DUSTY BAKER

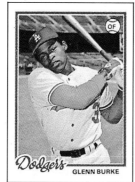

Dodgers — GLENN BURKE

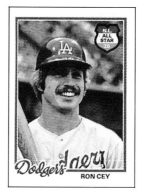

Dodgers — RON CEY

Dodgers — VIC DAVALILLO

Dodgers — TERRY FORSTER

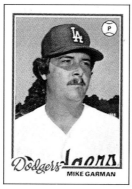

Dodgers — MIKE GARMAN

Dodgers — STEVE GARVEY

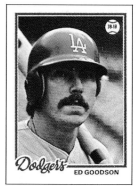

Dodgers — ED GOODSON

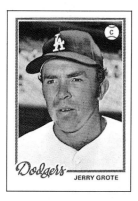

Dodgers — JERRY GROTE

Dodgers — BURT HOOTON

Dodgers — CHARLIE HOUGH

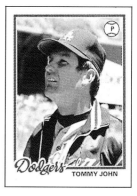

Dodgers — TOMMY JOHN

Dodgers — LEE LACY

AS MANAGER
TOM LASORDA
AS PLAYER
Dodgers

Dodgers — DAVE LOPES

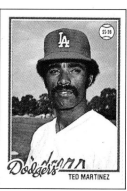

Dodgers — TED MARTINEZ

RICK MONDAY

MANNY MOTA

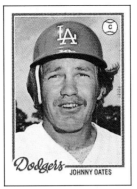
JOHNNY OATES

DOUG RAU

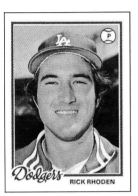
RICK RHODEN

BILL RUSSELL

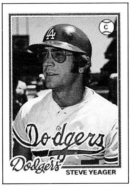
REGGIE SMITH

ELIAS SOSA

DON SUTTON

STEVE YEAGER

Dodgers

1979

Dreams of a third successive flag vanished quickly as the Dodgers finished in third place in the National League West.

At one point, five players were on the disabled list, and relief ace Terry Forster didn't rebound from off-season elbow surgery as expected.

The club led the league with 181 homers and Steve Garvey, Ron Cey and Davey Lopes each hit 28. The pitching staff was troubled for much of the year, but Rookie of the Year Rick Sutcliffe did go 17-10. Burt Hooton's 2.97 ERA was somewhat obscured by his 11-10 record. Don Sutton was 12-15. Andy Messersmith returned but his season ended in June when he required surgery. Doug Rau, who'd been consistent in recent seasons, was another who needed medical help.

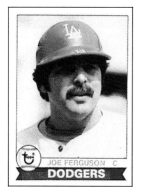

DUSTY BAKER OF
DODGERS

BOBBY CASTILLO P
DODGERS

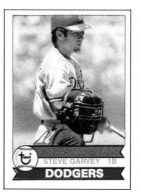

RON CEY 3B
DODGERS

VIC DAVALILLO OF
DODGERS

JOE FERGUSON C
DODGERS

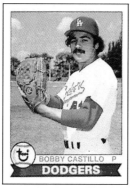

TERRY FORSTER P
DODGERS

STEVE GARVEY 1B
DODGERS

JERRY GROTE C
DODGERS

BURT HOOTON P
DODGERS

CHARLIE HOUGH P
DODGERS

TOMMY JOHN P
DODGERS

LEE LACY 2B-OF
DODGERS

DAVE LOPES 2B
DODGERS

TED MARTINEZ SS-3B
DODGERS

N.L. ALL-STAR
RICK MONDAY OF
DODGERS

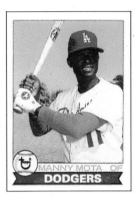

MANNY MOTA OF
DODGERS

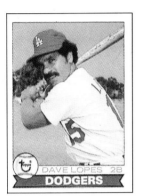

BILL NORTH OF
DODGERS

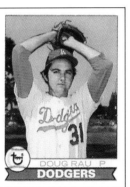

JOHNNY OATES C
DODGERS

DOUG RAU P
DODGERS

LANCE RAUTZHAN P
DODGERS

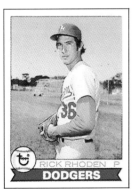

RICK RHODEN P
DODGERS

BILL RUSSELL SS
DODGERS

REGGIE SMITH OF
DODGERS

DON SUTTON P
DODGERS

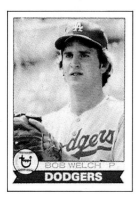

1980

The Dodgers, rebounding from their 1979 woes, missed winning the Western Division title in 1980 when they lost a one-game playoff to Houston after winning the last three games of the regular season to forge the tie.

Newcomers Dave Goltz and Don Stanhouse struggled.

Dusty Baker, Steve Garvey and Reggie Smith produced with the bat, but Baker slumped in September and Smith's problem shoulder betrayed him in mid-August.

Rick Sutcliffe's 3-9 record didn't ease the mound burden. Jerry Reuss, however, went 18-6 and Don Sutton, in his final Dodgers' season, was 13-5 with a 2.21. earned run average. Still, with all their injuries, the Dodgers drew three million in attendance for the second time in three years.

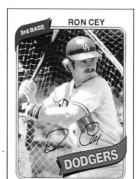

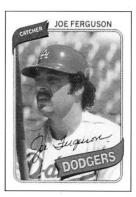

PITCHER TERRY FORSTER
DODGERS

1st BASE STEVE GARVEY ★N.L. ALL-STAR★
DODGERS

PITCHER BURT HOOTON
DODGERS

PITCHER CHARLIE HOUGH
DODGERS

OUTFIELD VON JOSHUA
DODGERS

PITCHER LERRIN LaGROW
DODGERS

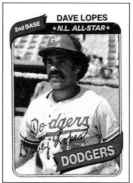

2nd BASE DAVE LOPES ★N.L. ALL-STAR★
DODGERS

SS-3B TED MARTINEZ
DODGERS

OUTFIELD RICK MONDAY
DODGERS

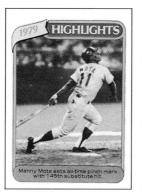

1979 HIGHLIGHTS
Manny Mota sets all-time pinch mark with 145th substitute hit.

OUTFIELD MANNY MOTA
DODGERS

CATCHER JOHNNY OATES
DODGERS

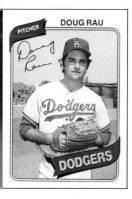

PITCHER DOUG RAU
DODGERS

PITCHER JERRY REUSS
DODGERS

SHORTSTOP BILL RUSSELL
DODGERS

OUTFIELD REGGIE SMITH
DODGERS

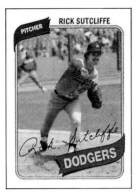

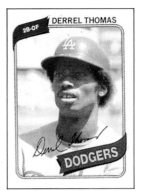
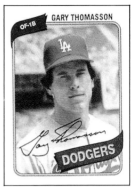

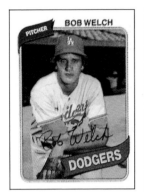

1981

In the strike-abbreviated 1981 season, the Dodgers, with Mexican left-hander Fernando Valenzuela winning both the Cy Young and the Rookie of the Year Awards, went all the way, winning the playoff and then defeating the Yankees in a six-game World Series.

Burt Hooton, 11-6, and Jerry Reuss, 10-4, combined with Valenzuela, who was 13-7 with a 2.48 ERA, and the trio was ably supported by a well-populated bullpen that got effective work from Dave Stewart, Steve Howe, Alejandro Pena, Tom Niedenfuer and Terry Forster.

Dusty Baker hit .320, while Steve Garvey batted .283. Pedro Guerrero, replacing the injured Reggie Smith, hit .300 with a dozen homers. Rick Monday, playing part-time, hit .315 and had the pennant-winning homer vs Montreal in the League Championship Series. Ron Cey, Guerrero and Steve Yeager shared MVP honors in the World Series.

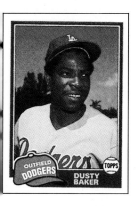

OUTFIELD
DODGERS
DUSTY BAKER

PITCHER
DODGERS
JOE BECKWITH

PITCHER
DODGERS
BOBBY CASTILLO

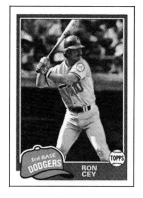

3rd BASE
DODGERS
RON CEY

CATCHER
DODGERS
JOE FERGUSON

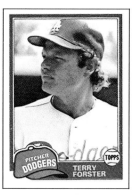

PITCHER
DODGERS
TERRY FORSTER

• N.L. ALL-STAR •

1st BASE
DODGERS
STEVE GARVEY

PITCHER
DODGERS
DAVE GOLTZ

OF-1B-3B
DODGERS
PEDRO GUERRERO

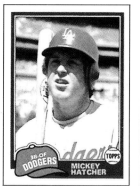

3B-OF
DODGERS
MICKEY HATCHER

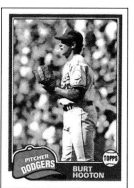

PITCHER
DODGERS
BURT HOOTON

PITCHER
DODGERS
STEVE HOWE

OUTFIELD
DODGERS
JAY JOHNSTONE

OUTFIELD
DODGERS
KEN LANDREAUX

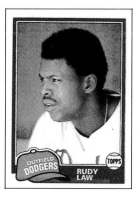

OUTFIELD
DODGERS
RUDY LAW

• N.L. ALL-STAR •

2nd BASE
DODGERS
DAVE LOPES

OUTFIELD DODGERS
RICK MONDAY

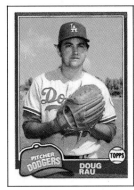

PITCHER DODGERS
DOUG RAU

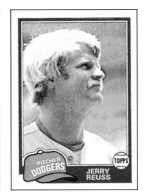

PITCHER DODGERS
JERRY REUSS

N.L. ALL-STAR
SHORTSTOP DODGERS
BILL RUSSELL

N.L. ALL-STAR
OUTFIELD DODGERS
REGGIE SMITH

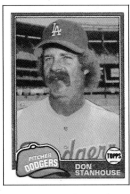

PITCHER DODGERS
DON STANHOUSE

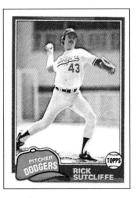

PITCHER DODGERS
RICK SUTCLIFFE

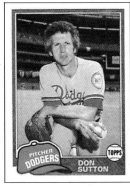

PITCHER DODGERS
DON SUTTON

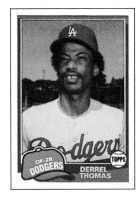

OF-2B DODGERS
DERREL THOMAS

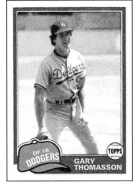

OF-1B DODGERS
GARY THOMASSON

PITCHER DODGERS
FERNANDO VALENZUELA

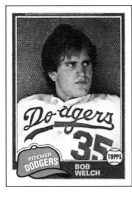

PITCHER DODGERS
BOB WELCH

CATCHER DODGERS
STEVE YEAGER

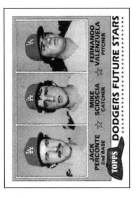

DODGERS FUTURE STARS
FERNANDO VALENZUELA PITCHER
MIKE SCIOSCIA CATCHER
JACK PERCONTE 2nd BASE

LOS ANGELES DODGERS
TOM LASORDA, MANAGER

1982

The Dodgers, after overcoming a sputtering start, just missed taking Western Division honors when they were nosed out by the front-running Braves on the season's final day. Steve Garvey and Ron Cey, who had their troubles in the early going, finished strong. Garvey hit 16 homers and knocked in 86 runs, while Cey had 24 homers and 79 runs batted in.

Pedro Guerrero did it all, batting .304 with 32 homers and 100 RBI. Dusty Baker wound up with 23 home runs, 88 RBI and a .300 average. Second baseman Steve Sax, with 49 stolen bases, was Rookie of the Year.

Fernando Valenzuela, rookie sensation of 1981, won 19. Jerry Reuss went 18-11 and Bob Welch finished at 16-11. The race produced another three million mark in home attendance for the Dodgers.

DODGERS
OUTFIELD DUSTY BAKER

DODGERS
SHORTSTOP MARK BELANGER

DODGERS
PITCHER BOBBY CASTILLO

DODGERS
3rd BASE RON CEY

RON CEY
in action

DODGERS
PITCHER TERRY FORSTER

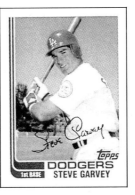
DODGERS
1st BASE STEVE GARVEY

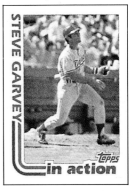
STEVE GARVEY
in action

DODGERS
PITCHER DAVE GOLTZ

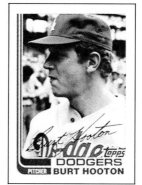

DODGERS
OUTFIELD PEDRO GUERRERO

DODGERS
PITCHER BURT HOOTON

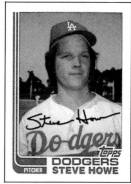

DODGERS
PITCHER STEVE HOWE

DODGERS
OUTFIELD JAY JOHNSTONE

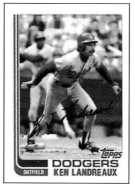

DODGERS
OUTFIELD KEN LANDREAUX

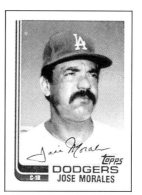

N.L. ALL STAR
2nd BASE DAVE LOPES

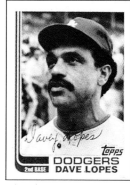

DODGERS
2nd BASE DAVE LOPES

DAVE LOPES
in action

DODGERS
OUTFIELD RICK MONDAY

DODGERS
C-1B JOSE MORALES

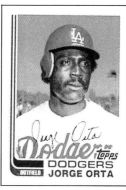

DODGERS
OUTFIELD JORGE ORTA

DODGERS
PITCHER JERRY REUSS

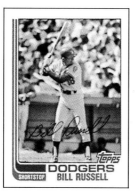

DODGERS
SHORTSTOP BILL RUSSELL

DODGERS
2nd BASE STEVE SAX

DODGERS
CATCHER MIKE SCIOSCIA

DODGERS
OUTFIELD   REGGIE SMITH

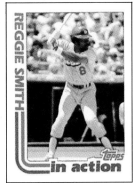

REGGIE SMITH
in action

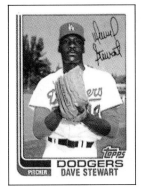

DODGERS
PITCHER   DAVE STEWART

DODGERS
PITCHER   RICK SUTCLIFFE

DODGERS
OF-2B   DERREL THOMAS

1981 HIGHLIGHT
FERNANDO VALENZUELA
Hurls 8 Shutouts as a Rookie

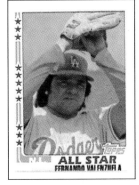

ALL STAR
FERNANDO VALENZUELA

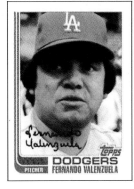

DODGERS
PITCHER   FERNANDO VALENZUELA

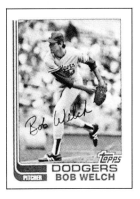

DODGERS
PITCHER   BOB WELCH

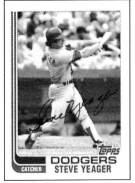

DODGERS
CATCHER   STEVE YEAGER

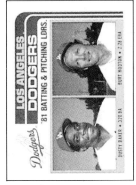

LOS ANGELES DODGERS
'81 BATTING & PITCHING LDRS.
DUSTY BAKER • .320 BA
BURT HOOTON • 2.28 ERA

LOS ANGELES DODGERS
FUTURE STARS
MIKE MARSHALL   1st Base
RON ROENICKE   Outfield
STEVE SAX   2nd Base

1983

The Dodgers captured another Western Division title in 1983, but fell to the East Champion Phillies in four games in the League Championship Series.

Pedro Guerrero, moving from the outfield to third base, hit .298 and had 32 homers and 103 RBI. Rookies Mike Marshall and Greg Brock did well. Marshall wound up at .284 with 17 homers. Brock had 24 homers despite hitting .224. Steve Sax batted .281.

Bob Welch, 15-12, had a 2.65 ERA and Alejandro Pena posted a 12-9 record. Jerry Reuss was 12-11 and Fernando Valenzuela finished at 15-10. Tom Niedenfuer, Pat Zachry and Dave Stewart manned the bullpen. Niedenfuer won eight and saved 11 while Zachry was 6-1. Stewart won five and saved eight others.

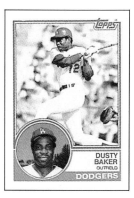
DUSTY BAKER
OUTFIELD
DODGERS

MARK BELANGER
SHORTSTOP
DODGERS

GREG BROCK
1st BASE
DODGERS

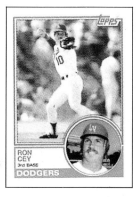
RON CEY
3rd BASE
DODGERS

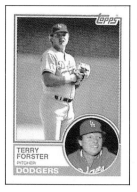
TERRY FORSTER
PITCHER
DODGERS

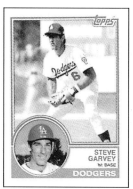
STEVE GARVEY
1st BASE
DODGERS

PEDRO GUERRERO
OUTFIELD
DODGERS

BURT HOOTON
PITCHER
DODGERS

STEVE
HOWE
PITCHER
DODGERS

RAFAEL
LANDESTOY
SS-2B
DODGERS

KEN
LANDREAUX
OUTFIELD
DODGERS

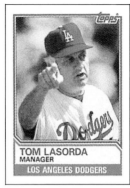

TOM LASORDA
MANAGER
LOS ANGELES DODGERS

MIKE
MARSHALL
1st BASE
DODGERS

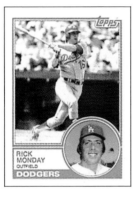

RICK
MONDAY
OUTFIELD
DODGERS

JOSE
MORALES
C-1B
DODGERS

TOM
NIEDENFUER
PITCHER
DODGERS

JORGE
ORTA
OUTFIELD
DODGERS

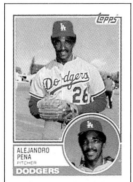

ALEJANDRO
PENA
PITCHER
DODGERS

JERRY
REUSS
PITCHER
DODGERS

RON
ROENICKE
OUTFIELD
DODGERS

VICENTE
ROMO
PITCHER
DODGERS

BILL
RUSSELL
SHORTSTOP
DODGERS

STEVE
SAX
2nd BASE
DODGERS

MIKE
SCIOSCIA
CATCHER
DODGERS

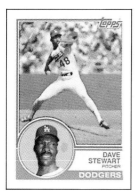
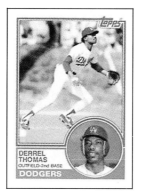

1984

Hitting woes dropped the Dodgers to fourth place with a record below .500 for only the second time since 1968.

Pedro Guerrero did bat .303 with 16 homers, but none of his teammates could put together an all-round season. Mike Marshall started well but knee injuries hindered him. Greg Brock, returned to the minors for a month, could do no better than .225.

Bright spots, however, appeared among the pitchers. Orel Hershiser was 11-8, and Alejandro Pena was 12-6 and his 2.48 ERA led the league. Bob Welch finished at 13-13 and Fernando Valenzuela was 12-17. Injuries in the bullpen also hurt with Tom Niedenfuer being out of action no fewer than four different times during the season.

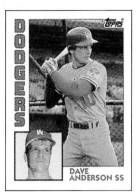 DAVE ANDERSON SS

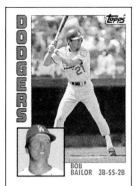 BOB BAILOR 3B-SS-2B

 DUSTY BAKER OF

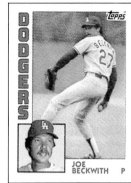 JOE BECKWITH P

 GREG BROCK 1B

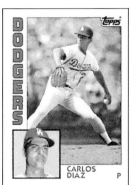 CARLOS DIAZ P

 JACK FIMPLE C

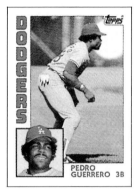 PEDRO GUERRERO 3B

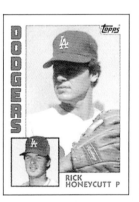 RICK HONEYCUTT P

 BURT HOOTON P

 STEVE HOWE P

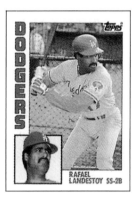 RAFAEL LANDESTOY SS-2B

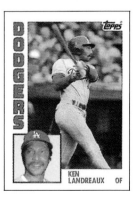 KEN LANDREAUX OF

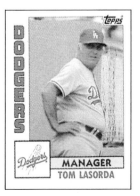 MANAGER TOM LASORDA

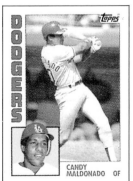 CANDY MALDONADO OF

 MIKE MARSHALL OF

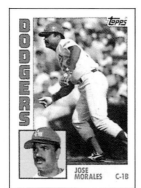
DODGERS
Topps
RICK
MONDAY OF

DODGERS
Topps
JOSE
MORALES C-1B

DODGERS
Topps
TOM
NIEDENFUER P

DODGERS
Topps
ALEJANDRO
PENA P

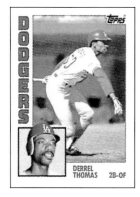
DODGERS
Topps
JERRY
REUSS P

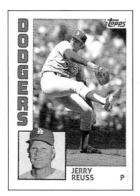
DODGERS
Topps
BILL
RUSSELL SS

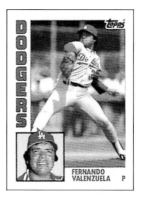
DODGERS
Topps
STEVE
SAX 2B

DODGERS
Topps
MIKE
SCIOSCIA C

DODGERS
Topps
DERREL
THOMAS 2B-OF

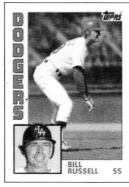
DODGERS
Topps
MIKE
VAIL OF

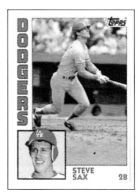
DODGERS
Topps
FERNANDO
VALENZUELA P

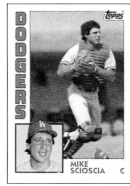
DODGERS
Topps
BOB
WELCH P

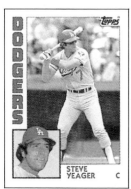
DODGERS
Topps
STEVE
YEAGER C

DODGERS
Topps
PAT
ZACHRY P

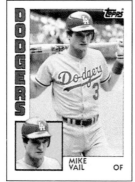

BATTING & PITCHING LEADERS
Topps
BOB WELCH
2.65 ERA
PEDRO GUERRERO
.298 BA
DODGERS

≡1985

Written off in the pre-season polls, the Dodgers won the Western Division by five and a half games over Cincinnati. However a defeat by the Cardinals in the League Championship Series prevented them from reaching the World Series.

Pedro Guerrero hit .320 with 33 homers and 87 RBI. Steve Sax wound up with a .279 average and Ken Landreaux batted .268 with a dozen homers. Greg Brock hit 21 four-baggers and catcher Steve Scioscia batted .296. Mike Marshall, despite a month off because of an appendectomy, hit .293 with 28 homers and 95 RBI.

The moundsmen didn't produce a 20-game winner, but a quartet posted ERAs below 3.00. Fernando Valenzuela, 17-10, was at 2.45 while Orel Hershiser went 19-3 with a 2.03. Bob Welch, bothered by arm problems, was 14-4 and 2.31. Jerry Reuss, 14-10, ended with a 2.92 ERA.

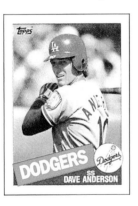

DODGERS — SS — DAVE ANDERSON

DODGERS — 3B-SS-2B — BOB BAILOR

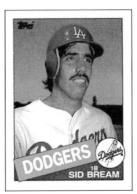

DODGERS — 1B — SID BREAM

DODGERS — 1B — GREG BROCK

DODGERS — P — CARLOS DIAZ

DODGERS — OF-3B — PEDRO GUERRERO

DODGERS — P — OREL HERSHISER

DODGERS — P — RICK HONEYCUTT

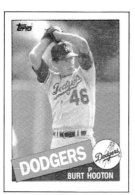

DODGERS
P BURT HOOTON

DODGERS
OF KEN LANDREAUX

DODGERS
MANAGER TOM LASORDA

DODGERS
OF. CANDY MALDONADO

DODGERS
OF MIKE MARSHALL

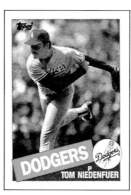

DODGERS
P TOM NIEDENFUER

DODGERS
P ALEJANDRO PENA

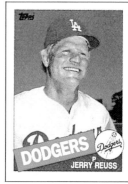

DODGERS
P JERRY REUSS

DODGERS
OF R. J. REYNOLDS

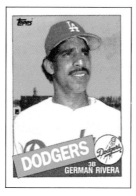

DODGERS
3B GERMAN RIVERA

DODGERS
SS BILL RUSSELL

DODGERS
2B STEVE SAX

DODGERS
C MIKE SCIOSCIA

DODGERS
OF-1B FRANKLIN STUBBS

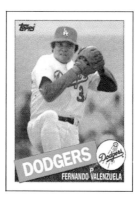

DODGERS
P FERNANDO VALENZUELA

DODGERS
BOB WELCH

DODGERS OF TERRY WHITFIELD

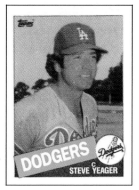

DODGERS C STEVE YEAGER

DODGERS P PAT ZACHRY

1986

The Dodgers toppled from the Western Division champions to fifth place. Despite finishing 16 games below .500, the club did draw more than three million customers at home.

Steve Sax was runnerup in the league batting race with a .332 average but the loss of Pedro Guerrero for virtually the entire season crippled the club's offense. Mike Marshall tried to pick up the power slack with 19 homers and 53 runs batted in. Fernando Valenzuela was manager Tom Lasorda's best pitcher, going 21-11 and leading the league with 20 complete games. Rick Honeycutt won 11 and lost nine while Orel Hershiser finished at 14-14.

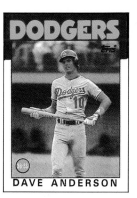

DAVE ANDERSON

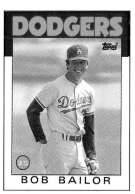

BOB BAILOR

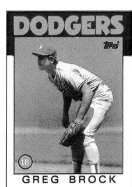

GREG BROCK

ENOS CABELL

DODGERS
P
BOBBY CASTILLO

DODGERS
P
BOBBY CASTILLO

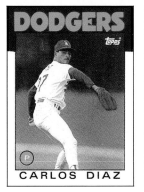

DODGERS
P
CARLOS DIAZ

DODGERS
2B-SS
MARIANO DUNCAN

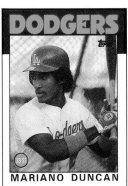

DODGERS
2B-SS
MARIANO DUNCAN

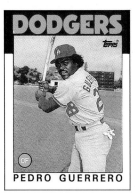

DODGERS
OF
PEDRO GUERRERO

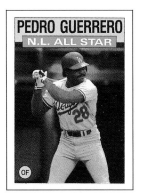

PEDRO GUERRERO
N.L. ALL STAR
OF

DODGERS
P
OREL HERSHISER

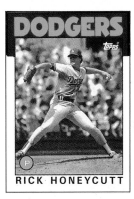

DODGERS
P
RICK HONEYCUTT

DODGERS
P
KEN HOWELL

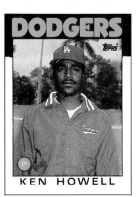

DODGERS
P
KEN HOWELL

DODGERS
OF
JAY JOHNSTONE

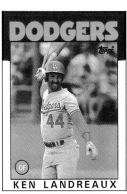

DODGERS
OF
KEN LANDREAUX

DODGERS
MGR
TOM LASORDA

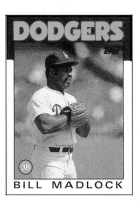

DODGERS
3B
BILL MADLOCK

DODGERS
OF
CANDY MALDONADO

MIKE MARSHALL

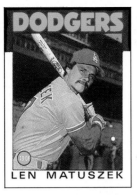
LEN MATUSZEK

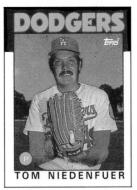
TOM NIEDENFUER

DODGERS OF-1B
AL OLIVER

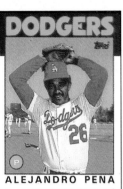
ALEJANDRO PENA

JERRY REUSS

BILL RUSSELL

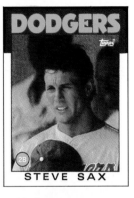
STEVE SAX

MIKE SCIOSCIA

'85 RECORD BREAKER
FERNANDO VALENZUELA, LOS ANGELES DODGERS
Most Consecutive Innings, Start of Season, No Earned Runs

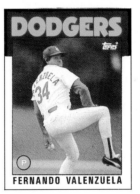
FERNANDO VALENZUELA

BOB WELCH

TERRY WHITFIELD

STEVE YEAGER

DODGERS LEADERS

1987

The Dodgers' second straight sub-.500 season in 1987 would have been even worse if it hadn't been for Tom Lasorda's pitching staff. Despite the fact that righthander Orel Hershiser was their top winner (16-16), Dodgers moundsmen pitched to a 3.72 ERA, second only to the division-leading Giants in the National League West.

As for the offense, Pedro Guerrero, idled virtually all of 1986 with a leg ailment, bounced back nicely. The Latin outfielder led the club with a .338 average, second best in the league. He also had 27 homers and 89 RBIs. John Shelby chipped in with a .277 average, plus 21 homers and 69 ribbies. Mike Marshall and Franklin Stubbs provided the Dodgers' remaining power. Marshall batted .294 with 16 home runs and 72 RBIs, while Stubbs, though hitting only .233, poked 16 homers and had 52 runs batted in.

In addition to Hershiser, Lasorda got a 15-9 season from Bob Welch, while Fernando Valenzuela finished at 14-14. The relief corps, however, was a bit of a problem. Alejandro Pena and lefthander Matt Young each posted 11 saves. Rick Honeycutt (2-12) and Tim Leary (3-11) had their woes. Rookies Shawn Hillegas (4-3) and Tim Belcher (4-2), both of whom worked late in the season, augured well for the Dodgers' pitching future.

DAVE ANDERSON

GREG BROCK

RALPH BRYANT

ENOS CABELL

MARIANO DUNCAN

PEDRO GUERRERO

JEFF HAMILTON

MICKEY HATCHER

BRAD
HAVENS

OREL
HERSHISER

BRIAN
HOLTON

RICK
HONEYCUTT

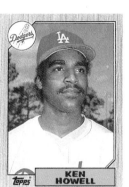

KEN
HOWELL

KEN
LANDREAUX

TOM
LASORDA

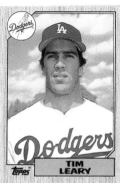

TIM
LEARY

BILL
MADLOCK

MIKE
MARSHALL

LEN
MATUSZEK

TOM
NIEDENFUER

ALEJANDRO
PENA

DENNIS
POWELL

JERRY
REUSS

BILL
RUSSELL

STEVE
SAX

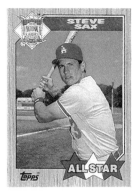

STEVE
SAX

ALL STAR

MIKE
SCIOSCIA

JOHN SHELBY

FRANKLIN
STUBBS

ALEX
TREVINO

FERNANDO
VALENZUELA

FERNANDO
VALENZUELA

ALL STAR

ED
VANDE BERG

BOB
WELCH

REGGIE
WILLIAMS

MATT
YOUNG

DODGERS LEADERS

1988

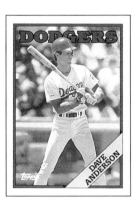

DODGERS

DAVE ANDERSON

Topps

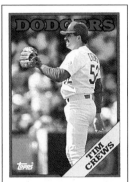

DODGERS

TIM CREWS

Topps

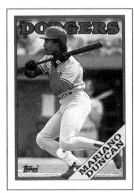

DODGERS

MARIANO DUNCAN

Topps

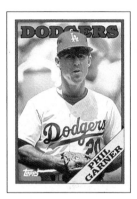

DODGERS

PHIL GARNER

Topps

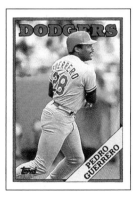

DODGERS

PEDRO GUERRERO

Topps

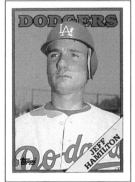

DODGERS

JEFF HAMILTON

Topps

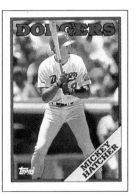

DODGERS

MICKEY HATCHER

Topps

DODGERS

BRAD HAVENS

Topps

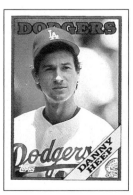

DODGERS

DANNY HEEP

Topps

DODGERS

OREL HERSHISER

Topps

DODGERS

SHAWN HILLEGAS

Topps

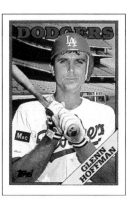

DODGERS

GLENN HOFFMAN

Topps

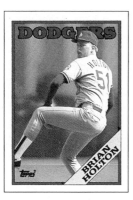

BRIAN HOLTON

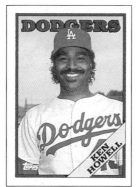

KEN HOWELL

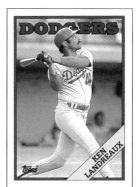

KEN LANDREAUX

TITO LANDRUM

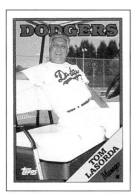

TOM LASORDA

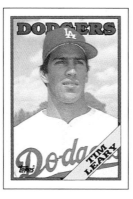

TIM LEARY

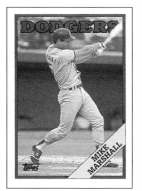

MIKE MARSHALL

LEN MATUSZEK

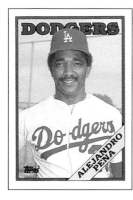

ALEJANDRO PENA

STEVE SAX

MIKE SCIOSCIA

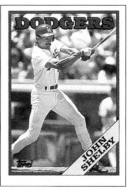

JOHN SHELBY

FRANKLIN STUBBS

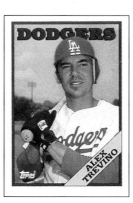

ALEX TREVINO

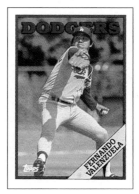

FERNANDO VALENZUELA

BOB WELCH

1951: Blue Back of Johnny Mize (50) lists for $25 . . . Red Back of Duke Snider (38) lists for $18 . . . Complete set of 9 Team Cards lists for $900 . . . Complete set of 11 Connie Mack All-Stars lists for $2750 with Babe Ruth and Lou Gehrig listing for $700 each . . . Current All-Stars of Jim Konstanty, Robin Roberts and Eddie Stanky list for $4000 each . . . Complete set lists for $14,250.

1952: Mickey Mantle (311) is unquestionably the most sought-after post-war gum card, reportedly valued at $6,500-plus . . . Ben Chapman (391) is photo of Sam Chapman . . . Complete set lists in excess of $36,000.

1953: Mickey Mantle (82) and Willie Mays (244) list for $1,500 each . . . Set features first TOPPS card of Hall-of-Famer Whitey Ford (207) and only TOPPS card of Hall-of-Famer Satchel Paige (220). Pete Runnels (219) is photo of Don Johnson . . . Complete set lists for $9,500.

1954: Ted Williams is depicted on two cards (1 and 250) . . . Set features rookie cards of Hank Aaron (128), Ernie Banks (94) and Al Kaline (201) . . . Card of Aaron lists for $650 . . . Card of Willie Mays (90) lists for $200 . . . Complete set lists for $5,500.

1955: Set features rookie cards of Sandy Koufax (123), Harmon Killebrew (124) and Roberto Clemente (164) . . . The Clemente and Willie Mays (194) cards list for $425 each . . .Complete set lists for $3,900.

1956: Set features rookie cards of Hall-of-Famers Will Harridge (1), Warren Giles (2), Walter Alston (8) and Luis Aparicio (292) . . . Card of Mickey Mantle (135) lists for $650 . . . Card of Willie Mays (130) lists for $125 . . . Complete set lists for $4,000 . . . The Team Cards are found both dated (1955) and undated and are valued at $15 (dated) and more . . . There are two unnumbered Checklist Cards valued high.

1957: Set features rookie cards of Don Drysdale (18), Frank Robinson (35) and Brooks Robinson (328) . . . A reversal of photo negative made Hank Aaron (20) appear as a left-handed batter . . . Card of Mickey Mantle (95) lists for $600 . . . Cards of Brooks Robinson and Sandy Koufax (302) list for $275 each . . . Complete set lists for $4,800.

1958: Set features first TOPPS cards of Casey Stengel (475) and Stan Musial (476) . . . Mike McCormick (37) is photo of Ray Monzant . . . Milt Bolling (188) is photo of Lou Berberet . . . Bob Smith (226) is photo of Bobby Gene Smith . . . Card of Mickey Mantle (150) lists for $400 . . . Card of Ted Williams (1) lists for $325 . . . Complete set lists for $4,800.

1959: In a notable error, Lou Burdette (440) is shown posing as a left-handed pitcher . . . Set features rookie card of Bob Gibson (514) . . . Ralph Lumenti (316) is photo of Camilo Pascual . . . Card of Gibson lists for $200 . . . Card of Mickey Mantle (10) lists for $300 . . . Complete set lists for $3,000.

1960: A run of 32 consecutively numbered rookie cards (117-148) includes the first card of Carl Yastrzemski (148) . . . J.C. Martin (346) is photo of Gary Peters . . . Gary Peters (407) is photo of J.C. Martin . . . Card of Yastrzemski lists for $150 . . . Card of Mickey Mantle (350) lists for $300 . . . Complete set lists for $2,600.

1961: The Warren Spahn All-Star (589) should have been numbered 587 . . . Set features rookie cards of Billy Williams (141) and Juan Marichal (417) . . . Dutch Dotterer (332) is photo of his brother, Tommy . . . Card of Mickey Mantle (300) lists for $200 . . . Card of Carl Yastrzemski (287) lists for $90 . . . Complete set lists for $3,600.

1962: Set includes special Babe Ruth feature (135-144) . . . some Hal Reniff cards numbered 139 should be 159 . . . Set features rookie card of Lou Brock (387) . . . Gene Freese (205) is shown posing as a left-handed batter . . . Card of Mickey Mantle (200) lists for $325 . . . Card of Carl Yastrzemski (425) lists for $125 . . . Complete set lists for $3,300.

1963: Set features rookie card of Pete Rose (537), which lists for $500-plus . . . Bob Uecker (126) is shown posing as a left-handed batter . . . Don Landrum (113) is photo of Ron Santo . . . Eli Grba (231) is photo of Ryne Duren . . . Card of Mickey Mantle (200) lists for $200 . . . Card of Lou Brock (472) lists for $75 . . . Complete set lists for $2,900.

1964: Set features rookie cards of Richie Allen (243), Tony Conigliaro (287) and Phil Niekro (541) . . . Lou Burdette is again shown posing as a left-handed pitcher . . . Bud Bloomfield (532) is photo of Jay Ward . . . Card of Pete Rose (125) lists for $150 . . . Card of Mickey Mantle (50) lists for $175 . . . Complete set lists for $1,600.

1965: Set features rookie cards of Dave Johnson (473), Steve Carlton (477) and Jim Hunter (526) . . . Lew Krausse (462) is photo of Pete Lovrich . . . Gene Freese (492) is again shown posing as a left-handed batter . . . Cards of Carlton and Pete Rose (207) list for $135 . . . Card of Mickey Mantle (350) lists for $300 . . . Complete set lists for $800.

1966: Set features rookie card of Jim Palmer (126) . . . For the third time (see 1962 and 1965) Gene Freese (319) is shown posing as a left-handed batter . . . Dick Ellsworth (447) is photo of Ken Hubbs (died February 13, 1964) . . . Card of Gaylord Perry (598) lists for $175 . . . Card of Willie McCovey (550) lists for $80 . . . Complete set lists for $2,500.

1967: Set features rookie cards of Rod Carew (569) and Tom Seaver (581) . . . Jim Fregosi (385) is shown posing as a left-handed batter . . . George Korince (72) is photo of James Brown but was later corrected on a second Korince card (526) . . . Card of Carew lists for $150 . . . Card of Maury Wills (570) lists for $65 . . . Complete set lists for $2,500.

1968: Set features rookie cards of Nolan Ryan (177) and Johnny Bench (247) . . . The special feature of The Sporting News All-Stars (361-380) includes eight players in the Hall of Fame . . . Card of Ryan lists for $135 . . . Card of Bench lists for $125 . . . Complete set lists for $1,200.

1969: Set features rookie card of Reggie Jackson (260) . . . There are two poses each for Clay Dalrymple (151) and Donn Clendenon (208) . . . Aurelio Rodriguez (653) is photo of Lenny Garcia (Angels' bat boy) . . . Card of Mickey Mantle (500) lists for $150 . . . Card of Jackson lists for $175 . . . Complete set lists for $1,200.

1970: Set features rookie cards of Vida Blue (21), Thurman Munson (189) and Bill Buckner (286) . . . Also included are two deceased players Miguel Fuentes (88) and Paul Edmondson (414) who died after cards went to press . . . Card of Johnny Bench (660) lists for $75 . . . Card of Pete Rose (580) lists for $75 . . . Complete set lists for $1,000.

1971: Set features rookie card of Steve Garvey (341) . . . the final series (644-752) is found in lesser quantity and includes rookie card (664) of three pitchers named Reynolds (Archie, Bob and Ken) . . . Card of Garvey lists for $65 . . . Card of Pete Rose (100) lists for $45 . . . Complete set lists for $1,000.

1972: There were 16 cards featuring photos of players in their boyhood years . . . Dave Roberts (91) is photo of Danny Coombs . . . Brewers Rookie Card (162) includes photos of Darrell Porter and Jerry Bell, which were reversed . . . Cards of Steve Garvey (686) and Rod Carew (695) list for $60 . . . Card of Pete Rose (559) lists for $50 . . . Complete set lists for $1,000.

1973: A special Home Run Card (1) depicted Babe Ruth, Hank Aaron and Willie Mays . . . Set features rookie card of Mike Schmidt (615) listing for $175 . . . Joe Rudi (360) is photo of Gene Tenace . . . Card of Pete Rose (130) lists for $18 . . . Card of Reggie Jackson (255) lists for $12.50 . . . Complete set lists for $600.

1974: Set features 15 San Diego Padres cards printed as "Washington, N.L." due to report of franchise move, later corrected . . . Also included was a 44-card Traded Series which updated team changes . . . Set features rookie card of Dave Winfield (456) . . . Card of Mike Schmidt (283) lists for $35 . . . Card of Winfield lists for $25 . . . Complete set lists for $325.

1975: Herb Washington (407) is the only card ever published with position "designated runner," featuring only base-running statistics . . . Set features rookie cards of Robin Yount (223), George Brett (228), Jim Rice (616), Gary Carter (620) and Keith Hernandez (623) . . . Don Wilson (455) died after cards went to press (January 5, 1975) . . . Card of Brett lists for $50 . . . Cards of Rice and Carter list for $35 . . . Complete set lists for $475 . . . TOPPS also tested the complete 660-card series in a smaller size (2¼" x 3 1/8") in certain areas of USA in a limited supply . . . Complete set of "Mini-Cards" lists for $700.

1976: As in 1974 there was a 44-card Traded Series . . . Set features five Father & Son cards (66-70) and ten All-Time All-Stars (341-350) . . . Card of Pete Rose (240) lists for $15 . . . Cards of Jim Rice (340), Gary Carter (441) and George Brett (19) list for $12 . . . Complete set lists for $225.

1977: Set features rookie cards of Andre Dawson (473) and Dale Murphy (476) . . . Reuschel Brother Combination (634) shows the two (Paul and Rick) misidentified . . . Dave Collins (431) is photo of Bob Jones . . . Card of Murphy lists for $65 . . . Card of Pete Rose (450) lists for $8.50 . . . Complete set lists for $250.

1978: Record Breakers (1-7) feature Lou Brock, Sparky Lyle, Willie McCovey, Brooks Robinson, Pete Rose, Nolan Ryan and Reggie Jackson . . . Set features rookie cards of Jack Morris (703), Lou Whitaker (704), Paul Molitor/Alan Trammell (707), Lance Parrish (708) and Eddie Murray (36) . . . Card of Murray lists for $35 . . . Card of Parrish lists for $35 . . . Complete set lists for $200.

1979: Bump Wills (369) was originally shown with Blue Jays affiliation but later corrected to Rangers . . . Set features rookie cards of Ozzie Smith (116), Pedro Guerrero (719), Lonnie Smith (722) and Terry Kennedy (724) . . . Larry Cox (489) is photo of Dave Rader . . . Card of Dale Murphy (39) lists for $8 . . . Cards of Ozzie Smith and Eddie Murray (640) list for $7.50 . . . Complete set lists for $135.

1980: Highlights (1-6) feature Hall-of-Famers Lou Brock, Carl Yastrzemski, Willie McCovey and Pete Rose . . . Set features rookie cards of Dave Stieb (77), Rickey Henderson (482) and Dan Quisenberry (667) . . . Card of Henderson lists for $28 . . . Card of Dale Murphy (274) lists for $5.50 . . . Complete set lists for $135.

1981: Set features rookie cards of Fernando Valenzuela (302), Kirk Gibson (315), Harold Baines (347) and Tim Raines (479) . . . Jeff Cox (133) is photo of Steve McCatty . . . John Littlefield (489) is photo of Mark Riggins . . . Card of Valenzuela lists for $7.50 . . . Card of Raines lists for $9 . . . Complete set lists for $80.

1982: Pascual Perez (383) printed with no position on front lists for $35, later corrected . . . Set features rookie cards of Cal Ripken (21), Jesse Barfield (203), Steve Sax (681) and Kent Hrbek (766) . . . Dave Rucker (261) is photo of Roger Weaver . . . Steve Bedrosian (502) is photo of Larry Owen . . . Card of Ripken lists for $12.50 . . . Cards of Barfield and Sax list for $5 . . . Complete set lists for $75.

1983: Record Breakers (1-6) feature Tony Armas, Rickey Henderson, Greg Minton, Lance Parrish, Manny Trillo and John Wathan . . . A series of Super Veterans features early and current photos of 34 leading players . . . Set features rookie cards of Tony Gwynn (482) and Wade Boggs (498) . . . Card of Boggs lists for $32 . . . Card of Gwynn lists for $16 . . . Complete set lists for $85.

1984: Highlights (1-6) salute eleven different players . . . A parade of superstars is included in Active Leaders (701-718) . . . Set features rookie card of Don Mattingly (8) listing for $35 . . . Card of Darryl Strawberry (182) lists for $10 . . . Complete set lists for $85.

1985: A Father & Son Feature (131-143) is again included . . . Set features rookie cards of Scott Bankhead (393), Mike Dunne (395), Shane Mack (398), John Marzano (399), Oddibe McDowell (400), Mark McGwire (401), Pat Pacillo (402), Cory Snyder (403) and Billy Swift (404) as part of salute to 1984 USA Baseball Team (389-404) that participated in Olympic Games plus rookie cards of Roger Clemens (181) and Eric Davis (627) . . . Card of McGwire lists for $20 . . . Card of Davis lists for $18 . . . Card of Clemens lists for $11 . . . Complete set lists for $95.

1986: Set includes Pete Rose Feature (2-7), which reproduces each of Rose's TOPPS cards from 1963 thru 1985 (four per card) . . . Bob Rodgers (141) should have been numbered 171 . . . Ryne Sandberg (690) is the only card with TOPPS logo omitted . . . Complete set lists for $24.

1987: Record Breakers (1-7) feature Roger Clemens, Jim Deshaies, Dwight Evans, Davey Lopes, Dave Righetti, Ruben Sierra and Todd Worrell . . . Jim Gantner (108) is shown with Brewers logo reversed . . . Complete set lists for $22.

1988: Record Breakers (1-7) include Vince Coleman, Don Mattingly, Mark McGwire, Eddie Murray, Phil & Joe Niekro, Nolan Ryan and Benny Santiago. Al Leiter (18) was originally shown with photo of minor leaguer Steve George and later corrected. Complete set lists for $20.00.

Pitching Record & Index

PLAYER	G	IP	W	L	R	ER	SO	BB	GS	CG	SHO	SV	ERA
AGUIRRE, HANK	477	1376	75	72			856	479	149	44	9	33	3.24
ALEXANDER, DOYLE	467	2708.1	160	135	1228	1117	1199	803	370	82	13	3	3.71
BECKWITH, JOE	214	403.2	18	19			306	144	5	0	0	7	3.39
BELCHER, TIM	No major league statistics												
BESSENT, DON	108	210	14	7			185	88	2	1	0	12	3.34
BILLINGHAM, JACK	476	2232	145	113			1141	750	305	74	27	15	3.83
BIRRER, BABE	56	119	4	3			45	37	1	1	0	4	4.39
BLACK, BUD	172	415	30	12			222	129	16	2	0	0	3.90
BRANCA, RALPH	322	1485	88	68			829	663	188	71	12	19	3.79
BRENNAN, TOM	52	187	8	7			95	35	16	2	1	5	3.90
BRETT, KEN	349	1526	83	85			807	562	184	51	8	11	3.93
BREWER, JIM	584	1044	69	65			810	360	35	1	0	132	3.06
BRUBAKER, BRUCE	2	3	0	0			2	1	2	0	0		15.00
BUNNING, JIM	591	3759	224	184			2855	1000	519	151	40	16	3.27
CADORE, LEON	192	1257	68	72			445	289	147	83	10	3	3.14
CALMUS, DICK	22	48	3	1			26	16	2	0	0	0	3.19
CASTILLO, BOBBY	250	688.1	38	40			434	327	59	9	1	18	3.95
CHIPMAN, BOB	293	880	51	46			322	386	87	29	7	14	3.72
COLLUM, JACKIE	171	464	32	28			171	173	37	11	2	12	4.15
CRAIG, ROGER	368	1537	74	98			803	522	186	58	7	19	3.82
CULVER, GEORGE	335	789	48	49			451	352	57	7	2	23	3.62
DABOLL, DENNIS	No major league statistics												
DIAZ, CARLOS	160	232.2	13	6			189	90	0	0	0	4	3.09
DOWNING, AL	405	2269	123	107			1639	933	327	73	24	3	3.22
DRYSDALE, DON	518	3432	209	166			2486	855	465	167	49	6	2.95
EGAN, DICK	74	101	1	2			68	41	0	0	0	6	5.17
ELSTON, DON	450	755.2	49	54			519	327	15	2	0	63	3.69
ERSKINE, CARL	335	1719	122	78			981	646	216	71	14	13	4.00
FARRELL, DICK	590	1704	106	111			1177	468	134	41	1	83	3.45
FERNANDEZ, SID	75	470.2	31	22	182	172	451	151	73	5	1	1	3.29
FITZSIMMONS, FREDDY	513	3225	217	146			870	846	426	186	30	13	3.51
FORSTER, TERRY	614	1105.1	54	65	454	397	791	457	39	5	0	127	3.23
FOSTER, ALAN	217	1028	48	63			501	383	148	26	4	0	3.73
FOWLER, ART	362	1025	54	51			539	308	90	25	4	32	4.02
GARMAN, MIKE	303	434	22	27			213	202	8	0	0	42	3.63
GIALLOMBARDO, BOB	6	26	1	1			14	15	5	0	0	0	3.81
GOLDEN, JIM	69	208	9	13			115	76	20	5	2	1	4.54
GOLTZ, DAVE	353	2038.1	113	109			1105	646	264	83	13	6	3.69
GRANT, JIM	571	2441	145	119			1267	849	293	89	18	53	3.63
GREGG, HAL	200	826	40	48			401	443	115	27	5	9	4.54
HARRIS, BILL T.	2	9	0	1			3	7	1	0	0	0	3.00
HATTEN, JOE	233	1087	65	49			381	492	149	51	7	4	3.87
HAUGSTAD, PHIL	37	57	1	1			28	41	2	0	0	1	5.53
HAVENS, BRAD	109	438	21	31	257	240	267	171	58	6	2	0	4.93
HERSHISER, OREL	124	668.2	44	25	255	212	465	210	89	25	10	5	2.85
HONEYCUTT, RICK	275	1562.1	87	105	750	673	649	453	244	46	10	1	3.76
HOOTON, BURT	480	2651.2	151	136			1491	799	377	86	29	7	3.38
HOUGH, CHARLIE	609	2168.2	131	115			1383	918	193	65	10	61	3.54
HOWE, STEVE	212	307	23	24			172	69	0	0	0	56	2.17
HOWELL, KEN	150	235	15	24	110	97	243	107	1	0	0	30	3.71
HUGHES, JIM R.	172	297	15	13			165	152	1	0	0	39	3.82
JENKINS, JACK	8	26	0	3			16	19	3	0	0	0	4.87
JOHN, TOMMY	684	4279.2	264	210	1781	1536	2083	1144	625	159	45	4	3.23
KEKICH, MIKE	235	860	39	51			497	442	112	8	1	6	4.59
KING, CLYDE	200	496	32	25			150	189	21	4	0	11	4.14
KIPP, FRED	47	113	6	7			64	48	0	0	0	1	5.10
KLIPPSTEIN, JOHNNY	711	1970	101	118			1158	978	162	37	6	66	4.24
KOUFAX, SANDY	397	2325	167	85			2396	817	314	137	40	9	2.76
KRUEGER, BILL	86	437.1	27	27	269	218	185	220	66	5	1	0	4.49
LABINE, CLEM	513	1080	77	56			551	396	38	7	2	96	3.63
LAGROW, LERRIN	309	778	34	55			375	312	67	19	1	54	4.12
LAMB, RAY	154	424	20	23			258	174	31	3	1	4	3.54
LASORDA, TOM	26	58	0	4			37	56	6	0	0	1	6.52
LEARY, TIM	61	288	17	20	153	131	180	84	45	4	2	0	4.09
LEE, BOB	269	492	25	23			315	196	7	0	0	63	2.71
LEHMAN, KEN	134	264	14	10			134	95	13	2	0	7	3.92
LEONARD, E. 'DUTCH'	640	3220	191	181			1170	737	375	192	30	44	3.25
LEWALLYN, DENNY	34	80.1	4	4			28	22	3	0	0	1	4.48
LOES, BILLY	316	1191	80	63			645	421	139	42	9	32	3.88
MAGLIE, SAL	303	1721	119	62			862	652	232	93	25	14	3.15
MARICHAL, JUAN	471	3506	243	142			2303	709	457	244	52	2	2.89
MARSHALL, MIKE G.	723	1386	97	112			880	514	24	3	1	187	3.15
MARTIN, MORRIE	250	604	38	34			245	251	42	8	1	15	4.29
McBEAN, AL	409	1072	67	50			575	365	76	22	5	63	3.13
McDEVITT, DANNY	155	456	21	27			303	264	60	13	4	7	4.40
McLISH, CAL	352	1609	92	92			713	552	209	57	5	6	4.01
MESSERSMITH, ANDY	344	2230	130	99			1625	831	296	103	27	15	2.86
MEYER, RUSS	319	1531	94	73			672	541	219	65	13	5	3.99
MIKKELSEN, PETE	364	653	45	40			436	250	3	0	0	49	3.38
MILLER, BOB L.	694	1552	69	81			895	608	99	7	1	52	3.37
MILLER, LARRY	48	145	5	14			93	57	20	1	0	0	4.72
MILLIKEN, BOB	61	181	13	6			90	60	13	0	0	4	3.58
MINNER, PAUL	253	1311	69	84			481	393	169	64	4	10	3.94
MOELLER, JOE	166	583	26	36			307	176	74	4	1	0	4.01
MOORE, RAY	365	1073	63	59			612	560	105	24	5	46	4.06
NEGRAY, RON	66	163	6	6			81	57	15	0	0	3	4.03
NEWCOMBE, DON	344	2155	149	90			1129	490	294	136	24	7	3.56
NEWSOM, BOBO	600	3758	211	222			2082	1732	483	246	30	21	3.99
NIEDENFUER, TOM	295	424	29	28	136	130	340	136	0	0	0	63	2.76
NORMAN, FRED	403	1938	104	103			1303	815	268	56	15	8	3.64
O'BRIEN, BOB	14	42	2	2			15	13	4	1	0	0	3.81
OESCHGER, JOE	365	1818	82	116			535	651	197	99	18	8	3.81
ORTEGA, PHIL	204	952	46	62			549	378	141	20	9	2	4.42
OSTEEN, CLAUDE	541	3460	196	195			1612	940	488	140	40	1	3.30
PALICA, ERV	246	839	41	55			423	399	80	20	3	12	4.23
PASCUAL, CAMILO	529	2930	174	170			2167	1069	404	132	36	10	3.63
PATTERSON, DAVE	36	53	4	1			34	22	0	0	0	2	3.13
PENA, ALEJANDRO	131	511.1	26	21	211	178	337	162	65	12	7	4	3.13
PENA, JOSE	61	112	7	4			82	58	1	0	0	5	4.98
PERRANOSKI, RON	737	1176	79	74			687	468	1	0	0	179	2.79
PODBIELAN, BUD	172	641	25	42			242	245	76	20	3	3	4.49
PODRES, JOHNNY	440	2265	148	116			1435	743	340	77	24	11	3.67
POSEDEL, BILL	138	679	41	43			227	248	87	45	4	6	3.72
POWER, TED	264	476.1	34	47	218	197	297	222	22	1	0	41	3.72
PURDIN, JOHN	58	111	6	6			68	52	5	1	1	0	3.89
RAKOW, ED	195	760	36	47			484	304	90	20	3	5	4.33
RAMSDELL, WILLARD	111	480	24	39			240	215	58	18	2	5	3.83
RAU, DOUG	222	1261	81	60			697	382	187	33	11	1	3.35
RAUTZHAN, LANCE	83	95	6	4			45	47	0	0	0	7	3.88
REED, HOWIE	229	516	26	29			268	208	35	3	1	9	3.72

PLAYER	G	IP	W	L	R	ER	SO	BB	GS	CG	SHO	SV	ERA
REGAN, PHIL	551	1373	96	81			743	447	105	20	1	92	3.83
REUSS, JERRY	537	3218.2	194	163	1438	1251	1744	1018	468	123	37	11	3.50
RHODEN, RICK	333	2118	121	97	903	818	1177	643	304	60	16	1	3.48
RICHERT, PETE	429	1166	80	73			925	424	122	22	3	51	3.19
ROE, PREACHER	333	1916	127	84			956	504	261	101	17	10	3.43
ROEBUCK, ED	460	790	52	31			477	302	1	0		62	3.35
ROMO, VICENTE	335	645.2	32	33			416	281	32	4	1	52	3.36
ROWE, KEN	26	45	2	1			19	14	0	0		1	3.60
ROWE, SCHOOLBOY	382	2219	158	101			913	558	278	137	22	12	3.87
RUTHERFORD, JOHN	22	97	7	7			29	29	11	4	0	2	4.27
SCHMITZ, JOHNNY	366	1813	93	114			746	757	235	86	16	19	3.54
SELLS, DAVE	90	130	11	7			49	67	0	0		12	3.91
SHANAHAN, GREG	11	23	0	0			13	9	0	0		1	3.52
SINGER, BILL	322	2174	118	127			1515	781	308	96	24	1	3.39
SMITH, JACK	34	49	2	2			31	17	0	0		1	4.59
SNYDER, GENE	11	26	1	1			20	20	2	0	0		5.54
SOLOMON, EDDIE	191	718	36	42			337	247	95	8	0	4	4.00
SOSA, ELIAS	601	919.1	59	51			538	334	3	0	0	83	3.32
SPECKENBACH, PAUL					No major league statistics								
SPOONER, KARL	31	117	10	6			105	47	16	4	3	2	3.08
STANHOUSE, DON	294	760.2	38	54			408	455	66	11	2	64	3.83
STEPHENSON, JERRY	67	239	8	19			184	145	33	3	1	1	5.72
STEWART, DAVE	247	766	39	40	367	337	484	310	72	9	1	19	3.96
STRAHLER, MIKE	53	159	6	8			80	79	13	2	0		3.57
SUTCLIFFE, RICK	251	1416.2	86	68	669	605	934	599	191	41	12	6	3.84
SUTTON, DON	723	5002.2	310	239	1959	1776	3431	1272	706	177	58	5	3.20
VALDES, RENE	5	13	1	1			10	7	1	0	0		5.54
VALENZUELA, FERNANDO	210	1554.2	99	68	589	507	1274	540	200	84	26	1	2.94
VAN CUYK, CHRIS	44	160	7	11			103	63	26	5	0	0	5.18
VANCE, SANDY	30	141	9	8			56	46	21	2	0	0	3.83
VANDE BERG, ED	332	409.2	22	26	191	168	256	168	17	5	0	20	3.69
WADE, BEN	118	371	19	17			235	181	25	5	0	10	4.34
WALL, STAN	66	98	4	6			55	35	0	0		1	3.86
WEBB, HANK	53	169	7	9			71	91	19	3	1	0	4.31
WELCH, BOB	257	1568.1	100	77	608	545	1096	479	232	41	19	8	3.13
WILHELM, HOYT	1070	2253	143	122			1610	778	52	20	5	227	2.52
WILLHITE, NICK	58	182	6	12			118	75	29	3	1	1	4.55
WILLIAMS, STAN	482	1763	109	94			1305	748	208	42	11	43	3.48
WRIGHT, RICKY	55	102.2	3	3	50	49	67	60	7	0	0	0	4.30
WYATT, WHITLOW	360	1762	106	95			872	642	210	97	17	13	3.78
YOUNG, MATT	157	639	37	48	352	309	421	258	94	12	4	14	4.35
ZACHRY, PAT	283	1165.	69	67			661	484	154	29	7	3	3.51
ZAHN, GEOFF	304	1848.2	111	109			705	526	270	79	20	1	3.74

Batting Record & Index

PLAYER	G	AB	R	H	2B	3B	HR	RBI	SB	SLG	BB	SO	AVG
ABRAMS, CAL	567	1611	257	433	64	19	32	138	12	.392	304	290	.269
ALCARAZ, LUIS	115	365	30	70	4	2	4	29	0	.260	21	58	.192
ALLEN, RICHIE	1749	6332	1099	1848	320	79	351	1119	133	.534	894	1556	.292
ALSTON, WALTER	1	1	0	0	0	0	0	0	0	.000	0	1	.000
AMOROS, SANDY	517	1311	215	334	55	4	43	180	18	.430	211	189	.255
ANDERSON, DAVE	351	926	118	210	35	4	9	69	31	.302	114	151	.227
ANTONELLO, BILL	40	43	9	7	1	1	1	3	0	.302	6	11	.163
ASPROMONTE, BOB	1324	4369	386	1103	135	26	60	457	19	.336	333	459	.252
AUERBACH, RICK	624	1407	167	309	56	5	9	86	36	.286	127	198	.220
BAILEY, BOB	1931	6082	772	1564	234	43	189	773	85	.403	852	1126	.257
BAILOR, BOB	955	2937	339	775	107	23	9	222	90	.325	107	164	.264
BAKER, DUSTY	2039	7117	964	1981	320	23	242	1013	137	.432	762	926	.278
BARBIERI, JIM	39	82	9	23	5	0	0	3	0	.341	9	7	.280
BAXES, JIM	88	280	39	69	12	0	17	39	1	.471	25	54	.246
BELANGER, MARK	2016	5784	676	1316	175	33	20	389	167	.280	576	839	.228
BERRES, RAY	561	1330	96	287	37	3	3	78	4	.255	134	134	.216
BILKO, STEVE	600	1738	220	432	85	13	76	276	2	.444	234	395	.249
BORKOWSKI, BOB	470	1170	126	294	43	10	16	112	2	.346	76	166	.251
BOYER, KEN	2034	7455	1104	2143	318	68	282	1141	105	.462	713	1017	.287
BRADLEY, MARK	90	113	13	23	5	1	3	5	4	.354	11	36	.204
BRAGAN, BOBBY	597	1900	136	456	62	12	15	172	12	.309	110	117	.240
BRANDT, JACKIE	1221	3895	540	1020	175	37	112	485	45	.412	351	574	.262
BREAM, SID	246	730	93	185	41	2	22	106	14	.422	86	108	.253
BREEDING, MARV	415	1268	154	317	50	5	7	92	19	.314	66	180	.250
BRIDGES, ROCKY	919	2272	245	562	80	11	16	187	10	.313	205	229	.247
BROCK, GREG	496	1506	195	351	53	2	71	219	19	.412	214	255	.233
BROWN, TOMMY M.	494	1280	151	309	39	7	31	159	7	.355	142	142	.241
BUCKNER, BILL	2176	8424	1008	2464	462	46	164	1072	175	.417	402	395	.292
BURKE, GLENN	225	523	50	124	18	4	2	38	35	.291	22	70	.237
BURRIGHT, LARRY	159	356	44	73	18	6	4	33	5	.295	22	92	.205
CABELL, ENOS	1688	5952	753	1647	263	56	60	596	238	.370	259	691	.277
CAMILLI, DOUG	313	757	56	153	22	4	18	80	0	.309	56	146	.199
CAMPANIS, JIM	113	217	13	32	6	0	6	34	0	.230	19	49	.147
CAMPANELLA, ROY	1215	4205	627	1161	178	18	242	856	25	.500	533	501	.276
CANNIZZARO, CHRIS	740	1950	132	458	66	12	18	169	3	.309	241	354	.235
CAREW, ROD	2469	9315	1424	3053	445	112	92	1015	353	.429	1018	1028	.328
CEDENO, CESAR	1969	7232	1079	2064	434	59	199	970	549	.445	657	925	.286
CEY, RON	2028	7058	965	1845	322	21	312	1128	24	.446	990	1203	.261
CHAPMAN, BEN	1717	6478	1144	1958	407	107	90	977	287	.440	824	474	.302
CIMOLI, GINO	969	3054	370	808	133	48	44	321	21	.383	221	556	.265
COLAVITO, ROCKY	1841	6503	971	1730	283	21	374	1159	19	.489	951	880	.266
COVINGTON, WES	1075	2978	355	832	128	17	131	499	7	.466	298	414	.279
COX, BILLY	1058	3712	470	974	174	32	66	351	42	.380	247	218	.262
CRAWFORD, WILLIE	1210	3435	507	921	152	35	86	419	47	.408	431	664	.268
CRUZ, HENRY	171	280	32	64	7	3	8	34	1	.361	25	31	.229
CUCCINELLO, TONY	1704	6184	730	1729	334	46	94	884	42	.394	579	497	.280
DARWIN, BOBBY	646	2224	250	559	76	16	83	328	16	.412	160	577	.251
DAVALILLO, VIC	1458	4017	509	1122	160	37	36	329	123	.412	212	422	.279
DAVIS, TOMMY	1999	7223	811	2121	272	35	153	1052	136	.405	381	754	.294
DAVIS, WILLIE	2429	9174	1217	2561	395	138	182	1053	397	.412	418	977	.279
DEAN, TOMMY	215	529	35	95	15	3	4	25	9	.242	42	105	.180
DEDEAUX, ROD	2	4	0	1	0	0	0	0	0	.250	0	0	.250
DEJESUS, IVAN	1348	4571	593	1162	175	48	21	323	194	.327	464	657	.254
DEMETER, DON	1109	3443	467	912	147	17	163	563	22	.459	180	658	.265
DIETZ, DICK	646	1829	226	478	89	6	66	301	4	.425	381	402	.261

PLAYER	G	AB	R	H	2B	3B	HR	RBI	SB	SLG	BB	SO	AVG
DRAKE, SOLLY	141	285	41	66	10	1	2	18	15	.295	32	53	.232
DRESSEN, CHUCK	646	2215	313	603	123	29	11	221	30	.369	219	118	.272
DUNCAN, MARIANO	251	969	121	231	31	6	14	69	86	.325	68	191	.237
DUROCHER, LEO	1637	5350	575	1320	210	56	24	567	31	.320	377	480	.247
EDWARDS, BRUCE	591	1675	191	429	67	20	24	241	9	.390	190	179	.256
EDWARDS, HANK	735	2191	285	613	116	41	51	276	9	.440	208	264	.280
ESSEGIAN, CHUCK	404	1018	139	260	45	4	47	150	6	.446	97	233	.255
FAIREY, JIM	339	766	86	180	28	7	7	75	6	.317	47	122	.235
FAIRLY, RON	2442	7184	931	1913	307	33	215	1044	35	.408	1052	877	.266
FERGUSON, JOE	1013	2951	407	719	121	11	122	445	22	.416	565	607	.244
FERNANDEZ, CHICO	856	2778	270	666	91	19	40	259	68	.329	213	338	.240
FERRARA, AL	574	1382	148	358	60	7	51	198	1	.423	156	286	.259
FIMPLE, JACK	66	174	18	42	9	1	2	25	1	.399	12	45	.241
FRANKS, HERMAN	188	403	35	80	18	2	3	43	2	.275	57	37	.199
FURILLO, CARL	1806	6378	895	1910	324	56	192	1058	48	.458	514	436	.299
GABRIELSON, LEN	708	1764	178	446	64	12	37	176	20	.366	145	315	.253
GALAN, AUGIE	1742	5937	1004	1706	336	74	100	830	123	.419	979	393	.287
GARNER, PHIL	1732	5885	751	1543	290	82	104	714	219	.392	535	795	.262
GARVEY, STEVE	2305	8759	1138	2583	438	43	272	1299	83	.448	478	993	.295
GENTILE, JIM	936	2922	434	759	113	6	179	549	3	.486	475	663	.260
GILLIAM, JUNIOR	1956	7119	1163	1889	304	71	65	558	203	.355	1036	416	.265
GOODSON, ED	515	1266	108	329	51	2	30	170	2	.364	83	135	.260
GRABARKEWITZ, BILLY	466	1161	189	274	41	12	28	141	33	.364	202	321	.236
GRAY, DICK	124	305	43	73	7	6	12	41	1	.420	33	52	.239
GRIFFITH, DERRELL	124	124	33	37	7	1	2	27	5	.378	7	33	.260
GROTE, JERRY	1421	4339	352	1092	160	22	39	404	15	.326	399	600	.252
GUERRERO, PEDRO	825	2842	448	865	137	21	139	461	75	.514	318	493	.304
GULDEN, BRAD	165	413	43	85	14	2	4	42	2	.286	42	56	.206
HAAS, BILL	No major league statistics												
HALE, JOHN	359	681	66	137	25	4	14	72	10	.305	43	183	.201
HALLER, TOM	1294	3935	461	1011	153	21	134	504	14	.414	477	593	.257
HAMILTON, JEFF	71	147	22	33	5	0	1	19	0	.361	0	43	.224
HAMRIC, BERT	10	9	0	1	0	0	0	0	0	.111	0	7	.111
HARKNESS, TIM	259	562	59	132	18	4	14	61	7	.356	58	118	.235
HATCHER, MICKEY	762	2543	269	715	133	5	25	270	8	.379	118	182	.281
HEEP, DANNY	560	1313	144	338	71	5	25	149	5	.376	153	175	.257
HERMAN, BILLY	1922	7707	1163	2345	486	82	47	839	67	.407	737	428	.304
HERMANSKI, GENE	739	1960	276	533	85	18	46	259	18	.446	289	212	.272
HERNANDEZ, ENZO	714	2327	241	522	66	13	2	113	129	.266	184	151	.224
HICKMAN, JIM	1421	3974	518	1002	163	25	159	560	17	.426	491	832	.252
HOAK, DON	1263	4322	598	1144	214	44	89	498	64	.396	523	530	.265
HODGES, GIL	2071	7030	1105	1921	295	48	370	1274	63	.487	943	1137	.273
HOFFMAN, GLENN	657	1872	223	462	95	9	22	191	5	.342	123	264	.247
HOLMES, TOMMY	1320	4992	698	1507	292	47	88	581	40	.432	480	122	.302
HOPKINS, GAIL	514	1219	142	324	47	6	25	145	4	.376	83	118	.266
HOPP, JOHNNY	1393	4260	698	1262	216	74	46	458	128	.414	465	378	.296
HOWARD, FRANK	1895	6488	864	1774	245	35	382	1119	8	.499	782	1460	.273
HOWELL, H. "DIXIE'	340	910	98	240	39	4	12	93	4	.337	87	140	.246
HUNT, RON	1483	5235	745	1429	223	23	39	370	65	.347	555	382	.273
HUTTON, TOM	952	1655	196	412	63	7	22	186	15	.334	234	140	.248
JACKSON, RANDY	955	3203	412	835	115	44	103	415	36	.421	281	382	.261
JAMES, CLEO	208	381	69	87	15	2	5	27	16	.318	52	52	.228
JOHNSON, LOU	677	2049	244	529	97	14	48	232	50	.389	110	320	.258
JOHNSTONE, JAY	1748	4703	578	1254	215	31	102	531	50	.394	429	632	.267
JOSHUA, VON	822	2234	277	610	87	31	30	184	55	.380	108	338	.273

PLAYER (continued)

PLAYER	G	AB	R	H	2B	3B	HR	RBI	SB	SLG	BB	SO	AVG
KELLERT, FRANK	122	247	25	57	9	3	8	37	0	.389	26	36	.231
KENNEDY, BOB	1483	4624	514	1176	196	41	63	514	45	.355	364	443	.254
KENNEDY, JOHN	856	2110	237	475	77	17	32	185	14	.323	142	461	.225
KOSCO, ANDY	658	1963	204	464	75	5	73	267	5	.394	99	350	.236
KRESS, RED	1391	5087	691	1454	298	58	89	799	47	.420	474	608	.286
LACY, LEE	1436	4291	615	1240	194	39	84	430	182	.411	340	608	.289
LANDESTOY, RAFAEL	596	1230	134	291	32	17	4	83	54	.300	100	123	.237
LANDREAUX, KEN	1149	3919	505	1062	176	45	85	456	140	.404	283	393	.271
LANDRUM, TITO	513	854	105	219	36	5	12	99	15	.367	71	160	.256
LARKER, NORM	667	1953	227	538	97	15	32	271	3	.390	211	165	.275
LASORDA, TOM							No major league statistics						
LAVAGETTO, COOKIE	1043	3509	487	945	183	37	40	486	63	.377	485	244	.269
LAW, RUDY	749	2421	379	656	101	37	18	199	228	.366	184	210	.271
LEE, LERON	614	1617	173	404	83	13	31	152	19	.375	133	315	.250
LEFEBVRE, JIM	922	3014	313	756	126	18	74	404	7	.378	322	447	.251
LEJOHN, DON	34	78	2	20	2	0	0	5	0	.282	3	13	.256
LEONARD, JEFFREY	862	2964	379	808	127	31	81	428	120	.418	221	618	.273
LILLIS, BOB	817	2328	198	549	68	9	3	137	23	.277	99	116	.236
LOPES, DAVE	1765	6311	1019	1661	230	50	154	608	555	.389	820	844	.263
LOPEZ, AL	1950	5916	613	1547	206	42	52	652	46	.337	561	538	.261
LUND, DON	281	753	91	181	36	8	15	86	5	.369	65	113	.240
LYTTLE, JIM	391	710	71	176	37	5	9	70	4	.352	61	139	.248
MADLOCK, BILL	1698	6207	859	1906	330	34	146	803	170	.442	571	460	.307
MALDONADO, CANDY	429	950	99	231	53	5	29	138	1	.401	64	167	.243
MANUEL, CHUCK	242	383	25	76	12	0	4	43	1	.260	40	77	.198
MANUSH, HEINIE	2009	7653	1287	2524	491	160	110	1173	114	.479	506	354	.330
MARSHALL, MIKE	575	1928	246	516	88	3	90	288	20	.456	161	474	.268
MARTINEZ, TED	657	1480	165	355	50	16	7	108	29	.309	55	213	.240
MATUSZEK, LEN	363	805	113	191	40	5	30	119	9	.411	87	164	.237
MAUCH, GENE	304	737	93	176	25	7	5	62	6	.312	104	82	.239
McMULLEN, KEN	1583	5131	568	1273	172	26	156	606	20	.383	510	815	.248
MICHAEL, GENE	973	2806	249	642	86	12	15	226	20	.284	234	421	.229
MIKSIS, EDDIE	1042	3053	383	722	95	17	44	228	52	.322	215	315	.236
MILLER, JOHN A.	32	61	4	10	1	0	2	5	0	.279	2	18	.164
MILLS, BUSTER	415	1379	200	396	62	19	14	163	24	.390	131	137	.287
MITCHELL, BOBBY VAN	202	617	75	150	15	8	3	43	9	.308	84	78	.243
MITCHELL, DALE	1127	3984	555	1244	169	61	41	403	48	.416	324	119	.312
MONDAY, RICK	1986	6136	950	1619	248	64	241	775	98	.436	924	1513	.264
MOON, WALLY	1457	4843	737	1399	212	60	142	661	89	.445	644	591	.289
MORALES, JOSE	733	1305	126	375	68	6	26	207	7	.408	89	182	.287
MORGAN, BOBBY	671	2088	286	487	96	11	53	217	18	.366	327	381	.233
MORYN, WALT	785	2506	324	667	116	16	101	354	7	.446	251	393	.266
MOTA, MANNY	1536	3779	496	1149	125	52	31	438	50	.389	320	320	.304
NEAL, CHARLEY	970	3316	461	858	113	38	87	391	48	.394	337	557	.259
NELSON, ROCKY	620	1394	186	347	61	14	31	173	7	.379	130	94	.249
NEN, DICK	367	826	70	185	35	3	21	107	1	.335	77	152	.224
NOREN, IRV	1093	3119	443	857	157	35	65	453	34	.410	335	302	.275
NORTH, BILL	1169	3900	640	1016	120	31	20	230	395	.323	627	665	.261
OATES, JOHNNY	593	1637	148	410	70	2	14	126	11	.313	141	149	.250
OLIVER, AL	2368	9049	1189	2743	529	77	219	1326	84	.451	535	756	.303
OLIVER, NATE	410	954	107	216	24	5	2	45	17	.268	72	172	.226
ORTA, JORGE	1734	5779	730	1610	263	63	128	741	79	.412	497	685	.279
PACIOREK, TOM	1365	4061	488	1145	229	30	83	491	55	.414	244	685	.282
PAFKO, ANDY	1852	6292	844	1796	264	62	213	976	38	.449	561	477	.285
PARKER, WES	1288	4157	548	1110	194	32	64	470	60	.375	615	613	.267
PASLEY, KEVIN	55	122	8	31	7	0	1	9	0	.336	6	13	.254
PERCONTE, JACK	409	1368	185	373	46	16	4	72	76	.334	138	113	.273
PIGNATANO, JOE	307	689	81	161	25	3	16	62	3	.351	94	116	.234
POPOVICH, PAUL	682	1732	176	403	42	11	14	134	8	.292	127	151	.233

PLAYER	G	AB	R	H	2B	3B	HR	RBI	SB	SLG	BB	SO	AVG
RAMSEY, MIKE	385	771	80	187	25	6	8	57	14	.298	46	107	.243
REESE, PEE WEE	2166	8058	1338	2170	330	80	126	885	232	.377	1210	890	.269
REISER, PETE	861	2662	473	786	155	41	58	368	87	.450	343	369	.295
REPULSKI, RIP	928	3088	407	830	153	23	106	416	25	.436	207	433	.269
REYNOLDS, R.J.	319	1034	136	278	57	11	15	125	46	.392	79	176	.269
RICHARDS, PAUL	523	1417	140	321	51	5	15	155	15	.301	157	149	.227
RIVERA, GERMAN	107	244	21	65	13	2	12	17	1	.361	17	32	.266
ROBINSON, EARL	170	421	63	113	20	5	12	44	7	.425	47	92	.268
ROBINSON, FRANK	2808	10006	1829	2943	528	72	586	1812	204	.537	1420	1532	.294
ROBINSON, JACKIE	1382	4877	947	1518	273	54	137	734	197	.474	740	291	.311
RODRIGUEZ, ELLIE	795	2173	220	533	76	6	16	203	17	.308	332	291	.245
ROENICKE, RON	450	961	128	238	47	2	16	104	23	.351	172	172	.248
ROJEK, STAN	522	1764	225	477	67	13	4	122	32	.326	152	100	.266
ROSEBORO, JOHN	1585	4847	512	1206	190	44	104	548	67	.371	547	677	.249
ROYSTER, JERRY	1287	3910	518	979	149	33	33	324	185	.331	382	486	.250
RUSSELL, BILL	2181	7318	796	1926	293	57	46	627	167	.338	483	667	.263
RUSSELL, JIM	1035	3595	554	959	175	51	67	428	59	.400	503	427	.267
SANDLOCK, MIKE	195	446	34	107	19	2	2	31	2	.305	38	45	.240
SAVAGE, TED	642	1375	202	321	51	11	34	163	49	.361	200	272	.233
SAX, DAVE	31	46	4	11	3	0	0	7	0	.304	3	3	.239
SAX, STEVE	774	3070	420	872	118	24	19	230	211	.357	274	294	.284
SCHOFIELD, J. DICK	1321	3083	394	699	113	20	21	211	12	.297	390	526	.227
SCIOSCIA, MIKE	665	1968	181	519	91	6	26	199	11	.346	288	130	.264
SHERRY, NORM	194	497	45	107	13	1	18	69	1	.346	37	102	.215
SHIRLEY, BART	75	162	15	33	4	1	0	11	0	.241	14	28	.204
SHUBA, GEORGE	355	814	106	211	45	4	24	125	5	.413	120	122	.259
SIMPSON, JOE	607	1397	166	338	54	12	9	124	45	.317	90	190	.242
SIMS, DUKE	843	2422	263	580	80	6	100	310	6	.401	338	483	.239
SIZEMORE, TED	1411	5011	577	1311	188	21	23	430	59	.305	469	350	.262
SKOWRON, BILL	1658	5547	681	1566	243	53	211	888	16	.459	383	870	.282
SMITH, CHARLIE	771	2484	228	594	83	18	69	281	7	.370	130	565	.239
SMITH, DICK	76	142	18	31	6	2	0	7	6	.289	6	42	.218
SMITH, REGGIE	1987	7033	1123	2020	363	57	314	1092	137	.489	890	1030	.287
SNIDER, DUKE	2143	7161	1259	2116	358	85	407	1333	99	.540	971	1237	.295
SPENCER, DARYL	1098	3689	457	901	145	20	105	428	13	.380	449	516	.244
STANKY, EDDIE	1259	4301	811	1154	185	35	29	364	48	.348	996	374	.268
STENGEL, CASEY	1277	4288	575	1219	182	89	60	535	131	.410	437	453	.284
STINSON, BOB	652	1634	166	408	61	7	33	180	8	.356	201	254	.250
STOCK, MILT	1628	6249	839	1806	270	58	22	696	155	.361	455	321	.289
STUART, DICK	1112	3997	506	1055	157	30	228	743	9	.489	301	957	.264
STUBBS, FRANKLIN	229	646	77	139	13	4	31	77	9	.392	61	173	.215
SUDAKIS, BILL	530	1548	177	362	56	7	59	214	9	.393	169	313	.234
SUKEFORTH, CLYDE	486	1237	122	326	50	14	2	96	12	.372	95	57	.264
TERWILLIGER, WAYNE	666	2091	271	501	93	10	22	162	31	.325	247	296	.240
THOMAS, DERREL	1597	4677	585	1163	154	54	43	370	140	.332	446	593	.249
THOMASSON, GARY	901	2373	315	591	103	25	61	294	50	.391	291	463	.249
THOMPSON, CHARLIE	187	517	49	123	24	2	8	47	2	.338	19	52	.238
TORBORG, JEFF	574	1391	78	297	42	9	8	101	3	.265	103	189	.214
TRACEWSKI, DICK	614	1231	148	262	31	9	8	91	15	.272	134	253	.213
TREVINO, ALEX	672	1876	192	467	81	8	15	186	13	.325	161	231	.249
VAIL, MIKE	665	1604	146	447	71	11	34	219	3	.400	80	310	.279
VALENTINE, BOBBY	639	1698	176	441	59	9	12	157	27	.326	140	134	.260
VALLE, HECTOR	9	13	1	4	0	0	0	2	0	.308	2	3	.308
VALO, ELMER	1806	5029	768	1420	228	73	58	601	110	.391	943	284	.282
VERSALLES, ZOILO	1400	5141	650	1246	230	63	95	471	97	.367	318	810	.242
WALKER, DIXIE	1905	6740	1037	2064	376	96	105	1023	59	.437	817	325	.306
WALKER, RUBE	608	1585	114	360	69	3	35	192	3	.341	150	213	.227
WALLS, LEE	902	2558	331	670	88	31	66	284	21	.398	245	470	.262
WALTON, DANNY	297	779	69	174	27	4	28	107	4	.376	88	240	.223

WASHINGTON, RON	461	1277	152	340	47	19	17	119	25	.373	55	212	.266
WELLMAN, BRAD	252	625	55	141	23	2	3	57	20	.283	45	114	.226
WERHAS, JOHN	89	168	15	29	3	2		14	0	.250	24	39	.173
WHITFIELD, TERRY	711	1899	233	536	93	12	33	179	18	.396	133	286	.282
WILLIAMS, DICK	1023	2959	358	768	157	12	70	331	12	.392	227	392	.260
WILLIAMS, REGGIE	150	312	39	87	14	2	4	32	10	.375	23	61	.279
WILLS, MAURY	1942	7588	1067	2134	177	71	20	458	586	.331	552	684	.281
WILSON, BOB	601	1763	206	455	84	8	24	189	25	.356	214	163	.258
WILSON, HACK	1348	4760	884	1461	266	67	244	1062	52	.545	674	713	.307
WINDHORN, GORDON	95	108	20	19	9	1	2	8	1	.333	11	19	.176
WYNN, JIM	1920	6653	1105	1665	285	39	291	964	225	.436	1224	1427	.250
YEAGER, STEVE	1269	3584	357	816	118	16	102	410	14	.355	342	726	.228
ZIMMER, DON	1095	3283	353	773	130	22	91	352	45	.372	246	678	.235